THE VISIBLE MISSION

ISBN
978-3-9824473-0-8 (hardcover)
978-3-9824473-1-5 (paperback)

Library of Congress Cataloging-in-Publication Data
Joubert, Henk
The Visible Mission: Business Success made Practical and Simple
1st Edition

Book design: Olivier Darbonville

THE VISIBLE MISSION

Business Success Made
Practical and Simple

Henk Joubert

FOR THOSE WHO CHANGE THE WORLD

Contents

Foreword

Given the apparently endless number of tools and toolboxes that promises to help you grow, transform, and evolved your business, which one do you use, and at what point?

This might be just one of the questions already on your mind, in addition to the pressing operational issues, the real fear of missing out on the next (BIG!) thing, new opportunities, or to deliver significant optimization from your limited resources.

It may also appear that you have freedom of choice from an endless number of opportunities for your business. However, the realistic options are very much constrained by the capabilities of your existing team, the maturity of your processes, and the relationships within your market. The glossy presentations tell us about awesome new business models, or new technologies with groundbreaking positive effects. You are promised improvements on both top- and bottom lines of your business, the ability to scale, numerous advantages and insights you will have, in addition to ease-of use. What you often are not told, is the real effort and potential delays in delivery and installation, the real total cost of ownership, and increasing dependencies, ending in severe vendor lock-ins.

What you are often being sold is the shiny tip of the iceberg where everything under the surface is ignored. The complexities and real, hard work needed within your organization is rarely mentioned. The reality is that the there is no magic; "it happens" by you and your team doing the hard, complex, and complicated work.

Digitalization isn't new, neither are the fundamental problems with how it is sold or approached within organizations. When I was doing software development on mid-range computers, working on wall-sized relational data models, we were already on the digitalization journey.

But even then, the basic flaw was that the work and technological development was often disconnected from the business. The basic mechanics to connect business outcomes with technology-based opportunities are often missing at most organizations. Now, years later – even with incredible developments like the internet, mobility, miniaturization, artificial intelligence - we see the same missing connective tissue.

It is exactly closing this gap that has driven me since my earliest experiences.

Leaders are invited to understand how digitalization can create real added value to the business. Digitalization is never just about a technology solution: we are not just converting an existing process or interaction into a technological, or digital version. Digitalization demands a change of mindset for you and your team. Most organizations approach digitalization with itself as the starting point.

Instead of using digitalization as the center of the universe, at Digital Innovation AG we make a Copernican shift: we start with our clients by looking at the business vision and goals. What are the real concrete outcomes that we are striving to deliver with the new solution? Where are the opportunities to optimize? How can we shape the solution to succeed today while we continuously build the foundation for tomorrow? Can we combine legacy solutions with digitalization to reach the target faster? We are looking for solutions that are pragmatic without sacrificing the flexibility needed to succeed in an ever-changing world.

There is no shortcut to digitalization. Shortcuts are high-risk endeavors – most of the time unsuccessful from a business point of view, and more expensive that you can imagine. Any savings that you think you will achieve by prematurely jumping into solutions, and implementations will leave you with vague and useless goals. You will have resource run-overs, missed deadlines, and underwhelming results. Even if you implement the solution, you are likely to have a brittle environment, leaving you in a permanent state of firefighting.

You will not only burn through resources, but also trust, goodwill from your team, and from your sponsors who will lose interest in supporting you. Instead of a healthy next-generation environment, you will be stuck with something sick and demanding, with no capacity to mature.

Therefore, digitalization needs your patience, your leadership and clear guidance to ask the right business questions first – of yourself, your team, and your partners. You need to own this. You need to lead by example. You are the one that will have to discover the business issues and opportunities, drawing on your experience, and that of your team. Nobody can solve these things from the outside with a "fixed price" or a "fast one-off". Not to the extent that you need it to succeed.

The Visible Mission offers you this guidance and places the control where it needs to be: in your hands. Henk's toolset is focused on exactly this. It provides you with full transparency and control over your business chances and risks, as well as the concrete action steps you need to take to grow, to evolve, and to transform where and when needed. This approach sums up how we at Digital Innovation AG are working "sleeves up" with the leaders and their teams with leading brands, and typical small and medium-sized businesses. This approach helps us to collaboratively solve our clients' concrete, real-world problems, delivering successful solutions.

The approach is:

- Presented in a very digestible and convenient way.
- Framed and delivered in your language.
- There is no new methodology which you need to understand.
- No new terms and acronyms you need to learn.

It is simply the combination of what you already know, placed in the right sequence and with a logical approach to keep you, with full overview, in the driver-seat. I hope you enjoy the ride of your company's life!

Christian Blümlein
Founder and Group CEO
Digital Innovation AG

Introduction

"You have to come to Conference Two right away," the nice lady from HR said.

It was the second Tuesday of April in 2012. I had been on a phone call with a software vendor when she peered over the wall of my cubicle, waving to get my attention.

Twenty minutes later, I walked out of the building having been laid off as part of a restructuring.

Restructuring, yes. The actual problem was that I failed as an enterprise architect. If I was bringing real value to the organization, they would have kept me. It wasn't a surprise to me: I was keenly aware of my inability to get technology decision makers to collaborate, which is exactly what I was hired to do.

I had a great product: lowering overall cost and increasing business agility through buying the right technologies and architectures. I had a customer: the multi-billion-dollar manufacturer that hired me for the job. But in the end, I was unable to show real and clear benefits or progress for the organization.

There was a disconnect between the executive that hired me and the people in the organization that I was supposed to work with. The business unit and department heads who were making the software buying decisions for their areas had little interest in considering their software's integration with other systems. They also had little interest in collaborating with other departments who were interested in acquiring the same type of solution.

In short, I had no market for my product. I did not understand the business model in which I found myself: it was similar to that of a non-government organization where you would be getting resources from one customer, working with a second, and delivering value to a third. I did not test my product nor consider innovative approaches: I simply kept going, doing the same, ineffective thing until I was laid off.

These are also the major reasons why most small businesses fail. Many will likely list these reasons – not the right product, not a market for the product, got beaten by the competition, or ran out of money.[1]

You may believe that hard work will ensure you succeed – you might be smart, have a good team, and know how to work hard. You might be a great developer, hacker, engineer, sales person, marketer, or even all of those. You may believe you can make it. Like the rest of us, you may also believe you are above average[2], and in many cases, you probably are. But even being above average is not enough.

Perhaps you think that it takes mostly luck to succeed – being at the right place at the right time. You may believe that you have to keep on swinging for the fences until you make it.

The reality is that success takes both hard work and luck. However, the "more you know, the luckier you get".[3]

It is not pure luck, and in some cases, no amount of hard work or amount of money will make you succeed.

For example, Segway was touted as a product that would change travel and even cities! It was designed by Dean Kamen, a highly successful designer. Over the years, Segway consumed millions of investment dollars. However, in the end, outside of large-city travel groups

---

1 Fundera, https:/www.fundera.com/blog/what-percentage-of-small-businesses-fail, link retrieved 20.1.2021.

2 Patrick Heck, https:/www.psychologytoday.com/au/blog/getting-along-and-getting-ahead/202001/people-think-theyre-better-average-how-much-better, link retrieved 11.1.2022.

3 A variation of a quote attributed by Gary Player to fellow golfer Jerry Barber.

and mall cops who used the product, there was no market for it. Segway finally closed down in 2020.[4]

ABOUT THE AUTHOR

The book is the result of trying things, and collecting learnings. Over my career I became increasingly frustrated with how poorly most businesses are run: a lack of coordination; seemingly daily changes in priorities; the same projects continuing even when strategies change; capabilities being developed that are not needed while critical ones are left weak, etc. The book in your hands is the result of processes and tools that I have found, developed, adapted, applied, and made work.

I started off as a software developer, before becoming a database designer, systems architect, project manager, enterprise architect, technology strategist, business architect, and finally business strategy developer.

I love designing and developing solutions, organizing data, and converting it to information that can be used to make better decisions. I had the opportunity to convert a decision support team into a team that created and built out a business intelligence platform. The original team was writing reports on demand as quickly as they could – however, the business intelligence team collaborated with power users to build a platform where the data was cleaned, and made available as prepackaged reports. These reports could be adjusted by the power users to create customized solutions to suit their own needs.

During my stint as business architect I worked closely with business strategists and planners, gaining good insights into why enterprise ar-

4 Fast Company, https:/www.fastcompany.com/90517971/exclusive-segway-the-most-hyped-invention-since-the-macintosh-to-end-production, link retrieved 11.1.2022.

chitecture[5] failed. It did so because it took a technology-driven, bottom-up approach but the real problem was the way the 'planning' was done, and how 'strategy' was implemented. Enterprise architecture failed even when we connected the business outcomes to the technology development.[6]

I did internal research interviewing organizational planners and leaders, and discovered that strategy development works at the executive level. However, the implementation of it mostly fails because of a lack of process, experience and tools within the organization. Strategy planning was a bureaucratic and mostly useless effort.

During my next assignment I figured out how the planning and funding process is at the root of the technology and process sprawl. The way goals and rewards, planning and funding was structured caused fragmentation and complexity. This fragmentation and complexity led to a fundamental inability to react effectively to changing business realities. Instead of developing better sails to move forward, we were building a bigger and heavier anchor, locking ourselves into a spot that was almost impossible to move away from.

While I knew way back when I started as an enterprise architect that the root of the fragmentation was not the fault of the technologists, I did not understand how it happened. Now I can only shake my head and think, "why did it take me so long to figure it out?".

To start filling these gaps between strategy, implementation plans, determining what is needed to succeed, monitoring progress, and knowing how to adapt to changing circumstances, I developed approaches and tools that I tested and implemented as we went along.

---

5 Enterprise architects have evolved from trying to understand, stop, and reverse the problems associated with 'legacy' solutions into more broad-based technologists - the way it is in 2020. My enterprise architecture work was focused on solving the 'legacy' problem.

6 Business architecture is the description of the business in terms of its capabilities, value streams, strategies, and structures.

WHAT YOU WILL LEARN IN THIS BOOK

The Visible Mission outlines a practical approach that will increase your chances of being 'lucky' in business – in other words, of being prepared at the right place at the right time with the right product.

You will see that there are plenty of things in business that are not luck, but a matter of knowing how to look, and how to understand what you see.

The approach I will share will help you to focus your always limited resources in the places where they will make a real difference. As the bee flying against a closed window would tell you if it could, not all hard work makes a difference.

The most valuable definition of strategy is a set of choices of where to engage[7] with our customers, and in which markets – those that play to our particular strengths.

I am going to show you that strategy management is accessible and fundamentally easy. It will need your time and attention, but the value you will receive will far outweigh your investment.

Strategy management is not rocket science: any reasonable person can do it. It is not voodoo: it is practical, applicable and useful.

I will help you identify and structure relevant information (most of which you very likely already have) in an easy-to-follow manner.

This information will become your mission control center.

I will also guide you through the process of developing an easy-to-repeat, goal-focused approach. This approach will turn your team into a focused entity working towards achieving your vision.

This book is very practical, with activities, and will show value fast.

It is presented in three parts:

---

7 Carl Von Clausewitz (*On War,* Book II, chapter 1) notes that strategy is "the use of engagements for the object of the war". In other words, strategy is a set of choices of where, when, and under which conditions to engage with the enemy. As businesses, our primary focus of engagement is with our customers – business strategy is the set of choices of where, when, and how to engage with our customers.

- Part I – Strategy Management: the Good (the benefits), the Bad (if you are not doing it), and the Busy (how the 'urgent' contributes to our failures).
- Part II – Strategy Management Made Easy: the What (introducing the Visible Mission approach in a hands-on manner) and the Why (i.e. why you should use it).
- Part III – The Making of your Moonshot (a structured, repeatable process to imagine, analyze, plan, execute, adapt and succeed).

For you to get the most out of *The Visible Mission*, I recommend you spend about 30 minutes daily on its key concepts. That includes constructing your mission control center. Ideally you will have some wall space where you can build your mission control center. An area of 2m x 2m (or 6 by 6 feet) will do nicely.

WHY SMALL AND MEDIUM ENTERPRISES/BUSINESSES (SMES)?

Firstly, large organizations can afford to pay the big bucks for the top consultancies, while that is not a practical solution for most SMEs.

Secondly, SMEs are responsible for the majority of employment and economic activity. Strengthening this part of any economy is therefore important for society. Successful SMEs are also a healthy way to counteract the concentration of wealth, and the growing inequality.

Thirdly, I believe strategy management can be made accessible to everyone. It is a practice - not black magic, nor wishful thinking. I believe CEOs and leaders can manage strategy without having to use a consultant. They are smart, know how to work hard, and want to succeed. Having spoken to numerous CEOs and leaders, I know that you know and understand your industry, your products, and your market segments. Managing strategy yourself lines up with your independent streak and can-do attitude as a CEO or leader. I believe that you are able to come up with creative and innovative solutions, not just for your products and services, but also with your business model, and your insights into your emerging future.

The Visible Mission is here to help you structure what you know, and identify what you need to know.

The fourth reason why this book focuses on SMEs is because I believe these organizations can and should play an active and leading role in social and environmental outcomes. SMEs combined have an enormous economic footprint. I believe that SME CEOs have a social and environmental responsibility as business leaders. They have an opportunity to improve the natural world and the society we leave to our children, and their children. I encourage you and your team to include social justice and environmental responsibility in your goals and metrics.[8]

The approach described in this book is a powerful tool. Use it with humility and responsibility.

It is for those who are interested in having a better chance at success, or a better fighting chance against your competition and surviving in a world that is changing faster than ever before. If a black swan is an unforeseen but major event[9], then we seem to be moving into a flock of black swans. (However, some of the things that are called black swans are nothing of the sort. Some black swan events have been predicted, but we might have chosen not to pay attention, or been unwilling to prepare for them. For example, the COVID-19 pandemic was foreseen and predicted after the SARS and MERS episodes.)

I don't know what the future holds any more than anyone else does. What I do know though is that the future usually reveals itself long before it floods us. Like climate change. Like digitization. Like a change in the current economic model.

---

8 See *Doughnut Economics: Seven Ways to Think Like a 21st-Century Economist* by Kate Raworth (2018) for a wonderful introduction to the principles behind this.

9 The black swan theory was developed by Nassim Nicholas Taleb and is described as an event that is unpredictable, with major implications. (See *The Black Swan: The Impact of the Highly Improbable*, 2007, Random House).

This book integrates the tools and approaches as *The Visible Mission*.

WHAT THIS BOOK IS NOT

This book is not about a particular industry, or a particular strategy that you should take. It contains no industry expertise outside of general business strategy, and a systematic approach to managing strategy.

This might NOT be the book for you:

- If you prefer to just 'wing' things;
- If you prefer to deal with the complexity of running a business and the associated risks by ignoring them;
- If you believe 'agile' means not having a plan, and changing work, goals and priorities all the time;
- If you believe goals are not something that can be achieved, or are too limiting, or they make you very nervous;
- If you prefer not to spend time planning, believing that it might cause you to miss new opportunities. This in turn will result in you adding work and overwhelming your team members by making them take on more and more;
- If you believe that listening to the insights of your team members is a sign of weak leadership, instead of inviting them to contribute to improving the organization;
- If you prefer to invest in new technologies without having an idea how to use them or to apply them to your products, channels, or capabilities,
- If you starve your team of critical resources;
- If you prefer to keep everyone in the dark, only issuing orders with no context;

- If you like to plan, but not monitor progress or adjust your plans;
- If you prefer not to know what trends might either put you out of business, or provide you with amazing opportunities;
- If you believe you know what is best for your customers without listening to them;
- If you prefer fixing symptoms because it is easier, cheaper, and faster than understanding what the underlying problems are and fixing those. Doing that only makes your business more fragile, and unable to adapt.

Now that we have explained what this book is and is not about, let's get into Part I!

PART ONE

Strategy Management: The Good, the Bad, and the Busy

You had an awesome idea, something that was going to change the world by solving some important problem that people were dealing with. You knew how to work hard, and you had a great team. You knew where the best markets were, and which capabilities you had to have in order to succeed. You were going to run a successful business because of its people.

CHAPTER 1

Why You Need Strategy Management Now

A local burger joint had a pretty good business going. Good burgers and beer (it was in Bavaria after all) in a small, cozy setup on the edge of the pedestrian zone, across from the main boulevard in town. There was no delivery, no pickup window, nor anything like that. Sure, you could order and get your burger to go, but who would want to do that if you can have it in such a great atmosphere? They had a single page website with a few pictures, the street address, a menu, the phone number, and an email address.

This coziness ended abruptly in March 2020 when the German government announced a 'hard lockdown'. Every non-critical business had to shut down and put the brakes on in what would turn out to be the first wave of the COVID-19 pandemic in Germany.

Food take-out and delivery businesses could still function. But Aschaffenburger was no McDonalds: it had no drive-through, and they had never had anyone even ask for a delivery before. They did not have anything in place to cater for take-out or delivery.

Out of nowhere, they were facing an existential threat.

They quickly decided to change their website, and update the menu, leading with a message that customers could by calling them or sending an email. As simple as that. My family and I decided to try them: we ordered, and our burgers were delivered. (Delicious.)

At the time of writing this book almost two years later, they are still in business. When the rules relaxed they collaborated with a neighboring pizza store to open a beer garden in the boulevard right across from them.

Their approach worked. It seems obvious and easy, but consider the fact that only 3 in 10 small and medium enterprises survive past their tenth anniversary. Even without a major event, like a pandemic! The restaurant across the street closed.

This is an example of how simple a good strategic move can be. Good strategy is not necessarily about high-tech, digitization, IOT, or big data. It could be, of course. But here was strategy in its glorious simplicity.

> **Hard work and commitment are not enough to survive, and to thrive in any business. Strategy management enables you to observe, evaluate, and decide where to focus your energy, time and resources. It also enables you to track and adjust effectively to changing realities in and around your organization.**

BUSINESSES ARE FAILING

According to data from Fundera[10]:

- 30% of small and medium enterprises (SMEs) fail by the second year,
- 50% fail by the fifth year, and
- 70% fail by the tenth year.

You may think you are above average and that you will make it. The reality is that we are not all above average, and most small businesses will not survive long-term without effective strategy management.

10 Fundera, https:/www.fundera.com/blog/what-percentage-of-small-businesses-fail, link retrieved 20.1.2021.

The reasons for business failures are simple: products without a market; better competition; running out of cash; a product that underperformed, etc. However, many of these reasons are knowable and/or testable in advance before spending a lot of time, money and energy.

The purpose of strategy is to enable us to identify and manage threats to our business' survival, and to identify and manage opportunities for success.

WHAT IS STRATEGY?

Strategy helps you to develop an organization with the capabilities needed to create customers (through a series of engagements) by providing them with products and/or services that they value. Strategy provides a pathway to the future.

Success[11] is a side-effect of doing this right.

Example: Apple created the iPhone, a device that combined the phone and the internet with a platform that delivers useful (and sometimes not so useful) apps to millions of people (who previously did not conceive or know that they might need something like it).

A vision helps to create direction and focus.

The core of strategy is understanding your customers, their needs, and the products and/or services that they find valuable. It is the choices of these customer markets that you will focus on, and where we can succeed.

A strategy is realistic only if you have the right capabilities in place. You need to know which capabilities you need at the right time. As you develop your capabilities over time, you continuously strengthen your organization. This capable organization provides more opportunities. to explore new potential customers, products and markets, enabling you to build success on success.

---

11 Financial success, but also social contribution and environmental conservation.

THE POWER OF STRATEGIC VISION

If you hope to inspire and guide our team towards creating a new future, you need to have a clear vision of that future. The vision creates the North Star that you can use to navigate and focus your efforts as a team. It enables you to create goals, plans and activities.

If you want to shape the future, you need to know how the world is developing and giving us a peek into the future now.

'Seeing' the Future

There is no magic crystal ball you can use to predict the future. However, there are always a number of major trends that indicate what is happening now, and how things may develop in the future.

For example, we see in 2022 that the share of electric vehicles is continuing to grow as a percentage of the market. There is no indication that trend will reverse. Therefore, if you are in the internal combustion engine business, then it is clear that the market as we know it is going to disappear. Naturally, this is a crisis for those manufacturers, but it is a visible, obvious crisis. It is therefore possible for those manufacturers to decide how to deal with it before it happens.

Similarly, the trend towards digitization is continuing with more products and services appearing every day. If your product/service can be digitized, it very likely will be soon. Either you can do it, or someone else will.

Strategy management enables you to be proactive to **prevent** preventable **crises**.

Even large businesses have failed because they either did not want to see, or could not see, what was coming. For example, Blockbuster was offered the opportunity to buy Netflix in 2000. However, the Blockbuster CEO declined, struggling to not openly laugh at the Netflix guys.[12] Blockbuster had an opportunity if they knew what to look for. Declining the Netflix offer was not just passing up an opportunity to grow beyond what they could imagine, it was also turning that opportunity into a threat. That threat turned out to be so significant that Blockbuster eventually failed and filed for bankruptcy in September 2010.

Testing Assumptions

Strategy management enables you to identify which **assumptions** about your strategies, customers, products, markets, plans and execution that you can and should test as quickly and inexpensively as possible.

It is critical to your success to know your customers' needs and pain points. These insights help you imagine and develop the solutions that they need and want. Strategy management helps you to clearly identify the **right products** and the **best market/s.**

For example, long before it became a streaming service, Netflix tested the assumption that people did not need a brick-and-mortar store to choose movies: they developed an online catalog that enabled its customers to pick the movies they wanted to watch and then have the DVDs conveniently mailed to them.

Strategy management guides you to systematically choose the right goals and projects, and help you to achieve them. It also helps you to AVOID choosing initiatives that are unlikely to contribute to your success.

Customer satisfaction is built into strategy management – you should know what your customers are thinking and feeling by listening closely and intently. A customer complaining may be the insight into the next product or service feature that you need.

---

12 Cnet.com, https:/www.cnet.com/news/blockbuster-laughed-at-netflix-partnership-offer/, link retrieved 11.1.2022.

Developing Your Team

Your strategy can only be executed if you have the right capabilities, usually in the form of your team and your partners. Strategy helps you to understand the **capabilities** needed to succeed in the markets we identify, and guides you in developing those capabilities.

Your vision and your choices for customer engagement help to identify what capabilities you have and those you may need to develop. Capability gaps can be closed through a combination of people, processes, technology tools and information.

A strengthened capability today gives you more options for picking tomorrow's strategies. It enables you to more quickly react to changing realities – the definition of agility.

You can even develop your capabilities and turn them into products. This is what Amazon did with their web services platform. They initially developed it for their own online retail platform, but then made it available to anyone who needed online, scalable computing facilities. Today Amazon Web Services brings in more money than the Amazon store.[13]

Focus

Insight-based planning is critical to create focus for your team. You can develop realistic plans for your business by:

- using your vision and ability to peek into the future,
- testing your assumptions about your strategies, customers, products, markets, plans and execution, and
- developing your team.

---

13 Peter Cohen, www.forbes.com/sites/petercohan/2020/01/06/how-much-of-amazons-73-billion-aws-profit-will-rivals-win/, link retrieved 11.01.2022.

Having focus will prevent wild changes in your priorities, since everyone will be clear on what should be done, and when. It also means that you will be in a better position to identify and ignore issues not relevant to your work. It prevents irrelevant crises and it helps to prevent your team from getting burned out with little to show for their efforts.

The vision and the plan create a sense of a common purpose – the vision is the moonshot you are working towards. Turning this vision into reality can create excitement among your team.

Without this sense of purpose, your team members are likely to lose their motivation, and you may see **sick leave** increasing. Some of your employees may tell you that they are **burning out** from having too much to do all the time. They may be turning over faster and faster. It is more difficult to **find employees** if your organization has developed a negative reputation.

The vision and the plan will focus your limited resources where it matters most. Strategic analysis and planning aren't going to bring money to the table on their own[14], but they help you understand where you should spend your limited resources.

For example, I worked with a team whose product was great, but they were spending very little resources on marketing, inhibiting their success. We reallocated resources, and they started landing more customers.

Working harder makes little difference if the activity is directed at the wrong place. Strategy management helps you to identify the relevant and decisive issues to work on.

Innovation

Strategy management also allows you to consider potential innovation opportunities across multiple areas of your business.

---

14 Although they may if you decide to merge your efforts with another organization.

- You can innovate your **business model**, like Netflix did by first shipping DVDs, then streaming, and later by developing their own content.
- You can innovate your **products** – making them awesome, like Apple did with the iPhone. (And if you throw in the app store and Apple Music, you have business model innovation on top of that.)
- You can innovate the way your product is **delivered.** For example, Rolls Royce leases their jet engines to airlines by the hour.
- You can innovate your own **capabilities**, like Amazon dies with their web services, as mentioned earlier.

> **Strategy is about identifying and managing both the threats to your organization, and the opportunities to thrive. Strategy management walks you through the critical aspects, and enables you to decide where to focus your limited resources. This will help you to succeed today, while you are also innovating and building the organization you need to thrive in the future. Vision, insights and plans create a common purpose and focus moving forward as we build a better world.**

As the example at the start of the chapter showed, Aschaffenburger survived by thoughtfully applying a strategy. They understood their situation, and came up with a relatively low-tech solution to make their business work in drastically changed circumstances. Strategy success is not determined by the flashiness of the execution; it's about identifying the right problem, making the right decisions, and executing the necessary actions. It's about choosing the best solution for the circumstance.

Aschaffenburger had no other option and they developed a 'good-enough' capability quickly enough. They spent their limited resources where it mattered. Their solution was easy to test, it was fast and cheap, and it worked.

You may already be well aware of most of the issues I have mentioned so far in the book. But you still may not be actively managing your strategy in your business. In the next chapter, we will look at reasons why strategy management often doesn't happen in organizations.

Your business is up and running, and you are making money, sometimes a lot of it. You are not always sure why or how, but it works, right! So why would you worry about strategy – your hard work and luck is working out great. Project planning is the only thing you need, the work is streaming in, and you are expanding your team. Anyway, planning is not your thing – you're agile, and planning will narrow your options so you won't be able to see new opportunities. Your issues are practical and planning or strategy does nothing to solve them. If the theory isn't enough, it's also difficult to figure it out. Sure, you can get a consultant, but why would you want to spend $2,000/day for a plan that goes on the shelf? You know your industry, your customers, and your products. Anyway, isn't strategic planning like trying to predict the future? It seems like something applicable only to large businesses.

CHAPTER 2

Why It's Likely You Are NOT Managing Strategically

Can you relate to any of the statements made above? If you're not actively managing your strategy, you are not alone. Few of your peers are doing it, despite its clear benefits.

In 1975, Kodak engineer Steven Sasson was awarded a patent for a digital camera. At that time Kodak was extremely busy, selling 90% of all camera film, and 85% of cameras.[15] In 1994, the Apple QuickTake 100 digital camera was introduced to consumers. It was developed with the help of Kodak.[16] In 1996, Kodak's revenue was $16 billion, and it was the 5th most valuable brand in the world. I cannot imagine how busy management was running such a successful business. In 2007, the Apple iPhone appeared, and it was also the year that saw the expiration of the original Kodak digital camera patent. Five years later, Kodak filed for bankruptcy.

---

15 Andrew Hudson, https:/www.photosecrets.com/the-rise-and-fall-of-kodak, link retrieved 11.01.2022.

16 Stewart Wolpin, https:/mashable.com/archive/digital-camera-20th-anniversary, link retrieved 11.01.2022

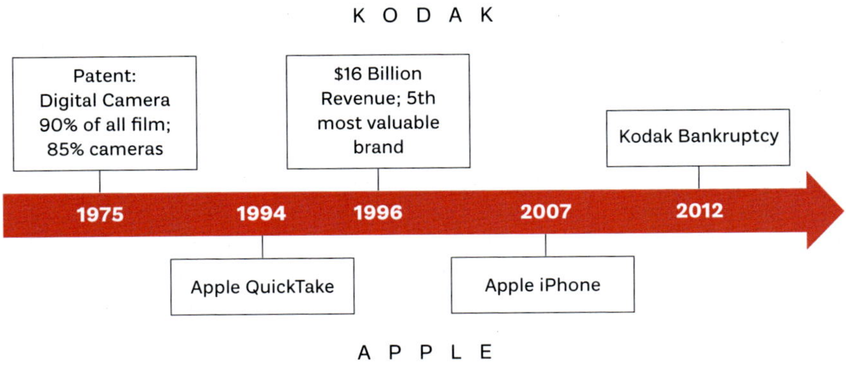

Figure 1 – An incomplete history of digital photography

Distracted by activity, Kodak missed what was happening. They were masters in film, cameras, photo paper and chemicals. Were the executives at Kodak distracted by focusing on the money they were making? It wasn't Apple's QuickTake or the iPhone that killed Kodak. The Kodak executives turned the opportunity of digital photography into a threat that they could not survive.

> **There are some understandable reasons why organizations are not managing strategically. These include an over-reliance on their own expertise or project planning alone, and their personal preferences. They also include misunderstandings and misconceptions about strategy management. For example, that it is theoretical, useless, too difficult, and/or expensive. There are also some legitimate criticisms.**

OVER-RELIANCE ON TECHNICAL EXPERTISE

You may find it weird that I'm writing a book about strategy management, since I'm a software developer by training, experience and passion. It's a lot more fun for me tinkering around, writing a new module or function, or developing a new database, class or UI than it is managing strategy. I love creating things, and creating new solutions!

Similarly if you are an engineer, you probably have a lot more fun designing, building and testing products, than you do managing. And if you are a salesperson, it's probably a lot more exciting talking to people, and showing them how your product or service is going to change their lives or their businesses.

When we have a passion, an aptitude and training, it's often a lot easier and fun to do than to think about the mission, the goals, the assumptions, the customers or the business models. I get it. I live that experience every day.

When the going gets tough, we instinctively turn to those things that we are highly skilled at. When 'stuff' happens, software developers code, engineers design, and marketers develop marketing plans, etc.

On top of that, planning on its own is not going to improve the product, sell the product, support customers, or do the marketing, etc. The practical work still needs to be done.

Does the following statement sound like you?

"To be very honest, I don't know how to 'do' strategy. I feel uncertain about getting involved in a process that isn't clear and easy for me to do. I doubt the value of doing it. Maybe at some level I am also afraid that it will force me to deal with issues that I have pushed into the background, because I don't really want to deal with them."

If it does sound like you, I understand. I have empathy.

But none of these feelings are an excuse for turning opportunities into threats, or allowing a threat to turn into a catastrophe.

OVER-RELIANCE ON PROJECT PLANNING

"I know how to plan a project (or how to set up and run sprints[17]), and that is enough."

It's great if you can effectively plan a project, but how do you know that it's the right project? Do you even know what a 'right project' means? Is it something that grows your business? In the right direction? With the right customers? With the right product or service? With the right capabilities? How do you know? Or do you simply take on anything that someone is willing to pay you for?

Strategy management helps you to define:

- what you want to achieve,
- how to approach it,
- what your viable options are,
- which customers to focus on,
- what products and services to offer, and
- what team and/or set of capabilities you need.

You can plan the perfect project, but if it's the wrong project, you will simply end up executing the wrong thing!

If project planning (or an agile process) is about doing the 'work right', then strategy management is about identifying the 'right work'. Strategy management is about identifying the best work to do, given your circumstances.

PERSONAL PREFERENCES

"Planning is not my thing."

If that's the way you feel, then you need to either make it your thing, or hire someone whose thing it is. The list of reasons why businesses

---

17 When done right, being agile will help you get important customer information built into your solution. But it still will not guarantee that your products or customers are the best options for your business to be working on.

fail are long, but most are preventable. Business failure can be prevented by identifying the right issue, acknowledging it, looking at what the options are, deciding on the right one (or ones), and then acting.

Strategic analysis and planning does not have to be drawn out, but it does have to be deliberate. Unless you are working completely on your own, you have to be able to communicate the intent of the plan coherently and effectively with your team.

If you can't hire someone to do it, I understand that as well.

I will show you throughout the book that strategy management is easier than you thought, and more fun.

Hang in there!

STRATEGY PLANNING IS THEORETICAL, MY PROBLEMS ARE PRACTICAL

This sounds like a reasonable complaint.

However, it's like builders saying they don't want the blueprint or the building plans because they are theoretical, and their work is practical. Strategy planning is all about solving practical problems, but crucially, it should identify the *right* practical problems to solve. It will in some cases also show you which problems *not* to solve – they may not be your problems, or they may only be symptoms, or things that lead you on a wild goose chase.

A director of enterprise architecture once told me about the practical urgency of consolidating six HR systems that his organization used globally. Only five minutes of questioning him made it clear to me that the problem was neither urgent (because the consolidation supported no business goal), nor practical (because the six HR systems were used in countries with different labor laws and tax codes). The only driver for consolidation was the theoretical enterprise architectural ideal of the simplified application landscape.

When done right, strategic management will also help prevent problems that are essentially theoretical.

STRATEGIES ARE USELESS – YOU DEVELOP THEM AND THEN THEY GO ON THE SHELF

I worked at an organization with business strategies that I thought were supposed to guide our activities and choices. When I made the case for a decision by referring to its alignment with our strategy, I was told by one of the executives that the strategies were 'just words'.

In my experience, even when strategies change, an organization's underlying projects remain – they just get justified using different arguments to match the new strategies.

None of what you will discover in this book is intended to go on the shelves, or be saved in some folder to be deleted in five years after being unused. The primary driver with *The Visible Mission* is to apply its relevant information.

You will be guided through strategic analysis, your options, your choices and the development of your plans. All of this key information will be obvious and visible. Your plans with firm goals will be tracked, and *The Visible Mission* will allow you to adapt as circumstances change, and guide you how to adapt.

STRATEGY PLANNING IS TOO DIFFICULT AND TOO EXPENSIVE

It was in the interest of a relatively small group of strategy consultants to present strategy management as a hyper-specialist occupation. [18] Ironically, this is also where strategic plans are typically delivered as a document through a presentation. Lots of money will change hands,

---

18 This does not mean that you could and should not use specialists when you need help. More detail about this later in the book.

and business will continue as before. The plans will go on the shelf.

I will be honest with you. During my career it also became clear to me that strategic planning is talked about a lot, but there is little understanding of what it is, and very little of it being done effectively.

There are some companies doing it, and some are doing it well, but it is the exception rather than the rule. It is sometimes done at the executive level, but then it will die in middle management. A strategic plan will be developed, and somehow all the projects that were planned before the strategy change will remain in place – they will now simply and plausibly align with the new strategies.

I also believe that as a CEO you know enough to develop your own strategies. I will place the easy-to-use tools in your hands, and you will be able to do it effectively yourself. As I mentioned in the Introduction to this book, strategy management is neither rocket science nor voodoo.

You are also likely to already be doing many of the components needed for strategic planning – you may simply not realize it, nor make the connections between the components clearly and consistently.

LEGITIMATE CRITICISMS OF STRATEGIC PLANNING (AND HOW *THE VISIBLE MISSION* IS DIFFERENT)

Recent research on strategy management[19] shows that as a practice, it is associated with higher revenues rather than cost savings.

However, there have been many legitimate criticisms leveled at strategy planning, and I mostly agree with them. I will stick to the major criticisms.

First of all, in many cases the working definition of strategic planning is to predict, plan, and execute. Henry Mintzberg[20] has criticized

---

19 *Does Strategic Planning Improve Organizational Performance?* George, Walker and Monster, 2019.

20 *The Fall and Rise of Strategic Planning,* Henry Mintzberg HBR.org, January-February 1994.

some of the fundamental practices of strategic planning. For example, we can't predict effectively, we can't detach strategies from operations, and we can't plan and then execute, because the planning often doesn't consider the realities when the execution takes place.

I agree with all of these criticisms.

The Visible Mission works in a fundamentally different way. We are not predicting. We are assuming and testing. The strategies and operations are intertwined like a double helix of DNA: we execute with an eye on the emerging reality, ready to adapt when necessary.

A quote from Mintzberg is that "strategic planning isn't strategic thinking. One is analysis, and the other is synthesis". Using these definitions, you will see that *The Visible Mission* brings these two distinct concepts together in a practical, highly visible way.

Roger Martin[21] added some of his own criticisms. These include that strategic plans are mostly large-scale initiatives, often without sharing the intent or the logic behind them. He also sees many strategic plans built on cost-based thinking, and suggests that business should plan for revenue instead. Finally, he criticizes the self-referential strategy frameworks, and explains that businesses are often too internally focused. This focus does not help these businesses convince their customers of their value propositions.

In the rest of the book you will see that this strategy management is not about large-scale initiatives. Instead it applies everywhere, with its context and logic obvious to everyone. Of course, *The Visible Mission* helps you to plan your organization's expenses, but it is primarily about enabling you to identify the best markets.

Finally, *The Visible Mission* walks you from the outside in: it focuses on what problems you want to solve for your customers, and then it ensures that you either have or can develop the necessary capabilities to do that.

---

21 *The Big Lie of Strategic Planning*, Roger Martin HBR.org, January-February 2014.

The Visible Mission has more in common with agile and lean practices than with the traditional predicting, planning and executing that some large corporations do. *The Visible Mission* acknowledges that goals and plans to achieve them are needed, but that as we are working towards that, we remain alert and ready to adjust and adapt as necessary. Not reflexively, but thoughtfully.

The Visible Mission involves doing our homework, preparing, playing to win[22], but being willing and able to change our strategy when change is the best response. The playing field will change over time. If we do it right, we will be the ones that will be changing both the playing field and the rules.

Even though there may be some legitimate criticisms of strategic planning, they don't negate the clear benefits of doing it. *The Visible Mission* makes strategy management easy, accessible, obvious, practical and fun.

Your organization's Visible Mission will develop over time, as the different elements are replaced with even better ones. You are also encouraged to adjust your organization's Visible Mission as you see fit. There was an absence of strategic thinking by the Kodak executives when it came to digital photography. They could not look at the information in the right context, or they were unable to synthesize it, as Mintzberg would probably say.

Without strategic management (thinking and planning), like Kodak you too are far more likely to miss both threats and opportunities. However, an even bigger barrier to strategic planning exists. That barrier is big enough to deserve its own very URGENT chapter. It's up next.

---

22 *Playing to Win: How Strategy Really Works,* A.G. Lafley, Roger Martin.

Speaking of practical matters, where would you find time anyway? My whole day, week and year is consumed by urgent matters. There are problems and potential opportunities everywhere that demand attention right away. Yes, I scheduled some strategy planning sessions, but I had to reschedule those. And again. After the fifth time, I canceled it. There was no point.

Anyone who has run a business will tell you a similar story. You need luck. And hard work. And 48 hours in a day.

But, when I'm really honest with myself, a lot of the urgent things that I spent time and energy on were absolutely wasted. But at the time, I had no way of knowing that. If only I did...

CHAPTER 3

The Busy: Urgent and Important

In his book, *The Checklist Manifesto*, Atul Gawande shows the checklist for the Cessna[23] when the engine stalls. This checklist is designed to enable the pilot to deal with this very critical and urgent problem.

The first entry is “Airspeed”.

The second entry is “FLY THE AIRPLANE”.

With a problem as challenging as the engine cutting out, the real risk is that the pilot will be so focused on restarting the engine that she/he may not pay attention to continuing to fly the plane. This may lead to it crashing, even though there are significant chances to bring it down safely. This risk is real even with experienced, professional aircrew.

On December 29, 1972 Eastern Air Lines Flight 401 crashed. The entire crew was distracted by a broken bulb on the front landing gear indicator. Having the front landing gear down is indeed an urgent matter, but it could have been checked manually. There was enough time and opportunity to do that. Sadly, they didn’t. Of the 175 people on board, 101 died.[24]

Gawande refers to such tunnel vision as cognitive overload.

---

23 A popular airplane.

24 *Eastern Air Lines Flight 401,* en.wikipedia.org/wiki/Eastern_Air_Lines_Flight_401, link accessed 22.01.2021.

This tunnel vision caused by urgency is also one of the reasons why CEOs don't manage strategy. In my discussions with CEOs, the single biggest comment about why they don't do strategic management is because they are too busy. This is understandable – as CEO, you are ultimately responsible for the success of your organization by understanding the situation you face and allocating resources to get the work done.

At any given time, there are thousands of things a business leader could be doing.

> **Our most limited and critical resource is our time and attention. Our natural reaction to urgent issues often wastes time, energy and resources, distracting us from the important. Left unchecked, this 'urgency tunnel vision' is likely to contribute to the failure of your business, and/or contribute to you missing valuable opportunities.**
>
> **The lack of strategy management is not only a symptom of urgency. It contributes to the flood of uncontrolled urgent matters because without strategy management, it is very difficult to know what is important, rather than urgent.**
>
> **While strategy management will consume your time and attention, you will get back far more than you invested.**

THE EISENHOWER MATRIX

The Eisenhower Matrix is useful to help us decide how we should allocate our attention and energy:

	Urgent	Not Urgent
Important	Do (extinguish, escape fire)	Schedule (e.g. buy food)
Not Important	Delegate (someone or something else's priority)	Do Nothing, Ignore

Figure 2 – The Eisenhower Matrix in theory

In theory, at least.

However, in practice there are two factors that have a major influence on the Matrix's effectiveness as a guiding principle. The first is our neurological, natural reaction to emergencies, and the second is when we don't have a dependable way to determine an issue or task's importance.

THE NEUROLOGY OF THE URGENT

We have two brain structures that allow us to function in the world.

Daniel Kahneman's[25] book *Thinking Fast and Slow* does a wonderful job of explaining the two systems – the fast, intuitive and the slow, deliberate systems. His research also shows how our quick, intuitive thinking is often profoundly wrong. The rational approach is more challenging, and takes more physical and emotional energy, but it leads to better decisions.

Walter Mischel, researcher and author of *The Marshmallow Test: Why Self-Control is the Engine of Success* calls these two systems the "hot" (intuitive) and the "cool" (rational).

The "hot" system is the emotional, the reactive and the immediate. In contrast the "cool" system is our prefrontal cortex, where we think rationally and slower. (It is this slowing down and engagement with the reality of a situation that allows us to make good investments for the future.)

When we are presented with an urgent situation, our natural reaction is to go into the hot, primitive way of acting where we want to deal with the situation as quickly as possible. There is nothing inherently wrong with us reacting in this manner: after all, it enabled humans to survive in the wild, escaping dangerous animals, etc.

---

25 Kahneman received the Nobel Prize for economics for his work on behavioral economics.

However, applying Mischel's approach to the Eisenhower Matrix makes it look more like this:

		HOT SYSTEM	COOL SYSTEM
		Urgent	Not Urgent
COOL SYSTEM	Important	**DO**	Schedule, reschedule
	Not Important	Delegate (someone or something else's priority)	Do Nothing

Figure 3 – The Eisenhower Matrix: neurological reflex

As we can see, in an emergency we develop a tunnel vision to deal with the perceived threat – like the Flight 401 crew that I mentioned at the start of the chapter.

To make things worse, when we do react to an emergency, we often experience an exhilaration of dealing with the event. We get another shot of endorphin. We feel great, on top of the world!

This puts us at risk of becoming emergency junkies who have no time for strategy management. However, jumping from one emergency to the next has a very damaging effect on an organization.

THE THREAT OF THE URGENT

Unfortunately, in many organizations there is also no clear way of determining what is actually important. When we don't know how to define what is important, the Matrix simplifies itself even further by assigning everything as important, or at best unknown, leaving us with only the urgent and non-urgent.

In practice, the Matrix then looks like this:

	Urgent	Not Urgent
Important (Priority Unclear)	**DO** (everything is a fire)	Schedule, Re-Schedule, Abandon

Figure 4 – The Eisenhower Matrix in practice

Because of this inability to identify what is important, the urgency of a task stands in as the deciding principle.

This breeds the next two crises:

1) Crisis solutions tend to be symptomatic fixes. And today's symptomatic fix is tomorrow's new crisis. Solving the symptoms creates another set of unintended consequences, causing the problem area to widen, and the environment to become more fragile.

2) Important issues that weren't urgent are ignored because of the urgent ones. And because there was no time, energy or a structured way to deal with them, they are often effectively ignored. They might have been issues like the competition introducing a new product, a provider developing closer collaboration with the competition.

Perhaps an important issue isn't a threat, but rather an opportunity that is missed – like Blockbuster missing the Netflix opportunity because they were too busy making money. In the same way that missed threats tend to hasten the demise of an organization, an exploited opportunity increases the ability to survive.

Is there a way for us to deal with this urgency-driven approach more appropriately?

DEALING WITH THE URGENT

Let's be honest, most of our day-to-day issues are not a matter of life and death. There are business crises, but most of the issues we deal with are not critical. Most of us have simply fallen into the habit of acting as if urgent means important, enjoying the rush of dealing with it successfully.

If there really is a life and death situation like an accident, fire, etc., then by all means deal with it urgently.

For everything else, I suggest the following.

When a seemingly urgent issue arises, say to yourself: "This issue is presented, or appears to me as an urgent matter." Doing that is a simple way of slowing yourself down and preventing you from reacting blindly.[26] The question about the situation will allow you to engage with it from a rational perspective.

The next thing to do is to ask: "How important is this matter? We know it isn't life and death, so does this constitute an existential threat? Does it constitute an opportunity to thrive? Is it a situation that will influence our current business, and our future business? Is it an issue with a customer, or a team member? Is it an issue about process, technology, or information?"

This will help us understand the actual situation better. We can also do the 'five whys' to get to the root of the issue.

Once you understand the situation, you can then decide whether it is something that you should address at all. Sometimes, people try intentionally (or unintentionally through misunderstanding) to make issues ours when they are not.

Once you have taken this more deliberate approach of evaluating whether what is presented is indeed an urgent issue, then you can legitimately ask yourself what the best time to react to the situation

---

26 This stepping outside of a perceived emergency activates the rational, objective, "cool" system. When that system is activated, the impulsive "hot" system is turned down or off.

would be. Does it need to be today? This week? This month? How about this quarter, or even this year?

You can also figure out if it's something that you should do, or whether you can delegate it to a team member or a partner.

At this point, you are in a much better position to address the right issues at the right time.

The Visible Mission provides you with a structure that enables you to work out for yourself what is truly important for your organization – your existential threats and opportunities. For you to succeed with your business, you need to manage your threats and opportunities. If you can figure out how to find and react to more opportunities, and learn to identify and appropriately react to threats, then you will greatly improve your chances of survival.

It does not mean that you won't still be busy. But there is another benefit that strategy management provides for you: it creates time.

CREATING TIME

What distinguishes elite athletes from the rest of us is not their ability to see faster than us.[27] We amateurs do it like this:

See	Act

Figure 5 – Amateur athletes

It is also not necessarily the ability to act faster than the rest of us, even though most elite athletes do, due to practice. The major distinction between them and us is that they are able to add a step in between the seeing and the acting: preparing. They are able to create a fraction of a second (in high speed sports like tennis) for themselves

27 *Wait – The Useful Art of Procrastination*, Frank Partnoy, 2012

where they get to interpret the information, and then decide whether to play deep, wide, short, etc.

See	Prepare	Act

Figure 6 – Professional athletes

The stakes are considerably higher for fighter pilots. They are trained to do something very similar, and being the military, there is an acronym for it: OODA[28] observe, orient, decide, act.

Observe	Orient	Decide	Act

Figure 7 – Fighter pilots (OODA)

The Visible Mission will help you to observe because its framework will ask questions which you might not have thought to ask before. For example, being more open to emerging trends. In addition, it will also help you to place information – like a random news report – into better context. For example, you might have heard that the disposable income in a market that you considered non-viable is increasing. 'Placement' and understanding of this information is part of what the fighter pilots call 'orient'. For our purposes, the term 'contextualize' may make more sense.

It will also provide you with a goal-based evaluation process to develop and strengthen your organization by improving your capabilities. These improved capabilities should enable you to react faster and more sure-footedly when confronted with opportunities or threats.

The visual and immersive nature of *The Visible Mission* allows you to observe and sometimes actively look for relevant information. Its

28 Developed by USAF Colonel John Boyd following exposure during the Korean and Vietnam Wars.

visual nature makes it a lot easier to orient yourself and your team. Once that is done, the decisions are not only easier, they are also more likely to be the better choices. Acting becomes focused, effective and efficient.

Although *The Visible Mission* is going to take the time that you will invest in it, it will create time for you – it will provide you with an 'early warning system', so to speak. You will 'see' much better, and you will also be able to prepare to act appropriately (as you will also be guided to develop the right skills in time.)

At this point you may be thinking: OK, the emergencies might kill me. But what does that have to do with strategy management in general, and *The Visible Mission* in particular?

I'm glad you asked!

The Visible Mission will help you analyze and plan your efforts to create customers and build your organization. It will provide you with the tools to understand your organization better, as well as the environment within which you operate.

Together these plans and tools will help you place events, demands, opportunities, and apparent and real emergencies in their proper context – quickly, rationally and effectively.

THE URGENCY OF STRATEGY MANAGEMENT

It seems on the surface that existential threats are long-term issues, and we have time to react to them. Electric vehicles, climate change – we have time. Not everything that looks like a threat is in fact going to turn into a business-killing event, is it?

Consider what Clayton Christensen calls "down-market innovation".[29] By the time the threat starts to get real, it's often too late for incumbents to react to it effectively. He explains how the big, tradi-

29 *The Innovator's Dilemma,* Clayton Christensen, Harvard Business Review Press, 2016.

tional steel producers were outplayed by the arc-furnace producers, who initially could only produce steel that the traditional producers considered to be low-margin. However, the arc-furnace producers managed to improve their process as they captured low-end market by low-end market. They didn't just have a different way of producing steel, they also had a different business model. By the time they started competing with the up-market products, the traditional producers were essentially outplayed. They did not have the capabilities, the experience, or the right business models.

The threat was never important to them, they always had time. They were making money.

Netflix was never important for Blockbuster. Until it was too late.

The internal combustion engine auto manufacturers are probably also thinking that they have time. That they will slap electric engines and batteries on their cars, and all will be good. But pay very close attention to what Tesla is doing. The way they produce their vehicles, the charging stations, the battery technology, the upgrades of their vehicles, the stripping away of dealerships, and the vehicle maintenance. The vehicle business model is changing – just adding electric motors and batteries will not be enough for the traditional manufacturers. I assume that there are arguments being made within the executive suites that the electric automobiles will cannibalize the existing models. Margins will be smaller. All true, but all short-sighted.

It might be useful to consider what McKinsey[30] describes as the four phases of digital disruption (as the same pattern is true for non-digital disruptions):

1) detectable (with lots of noise),
2) clear (the new business model is validated),

30 McKinsey, https://www.mckinsey.com/business-functions/strategy-and-corporate-finance/our-insights/an-incumbents-guide-to-digital-disruption, link retrieved 11.01.2022

3) inevitable (critical adoption mass achieved), and
4) the new normal (the new business model is scaled and becomes mature).

The critical point is when the business model is validated. This is when its viability is proven, and the adoption of it then usually moves quite fast. Incumbent businesses using the old business model see the 'oxygen' being sucked out of their markets. They face the dual challenges of dropping revenue, while having to take on the very difficult and expensive task of adapting to a changing market (including trying to fund necessary changes).

There is the quote from Hemingway's *The Sun Also Rises*: "How did you go bankrupt? Two ways. Gradually, then suddenly".

That is how it is with businesses failing.

Jeff Bezos has shared that Amazon had two years' head-start with Amazon.com, the Kindle, and the Echo.[31] It took their competition on average two years to catch up.

If your competition remains two years ahead of you, they remain one product cycle ahead of you. Each time you are under more pressure to react – figuring out how to respond, what the business model needs to look like, and if you have the right capabilities. If you have a competitor like Apple, it may force you out of the market completely – think BlackBerry.

Instead of trying to catch up, you could use strategy management to find ways to get ahead of your competition by developing and deploying new products and services before them. Like Amazon, this will give you an uncontested market for a while. And it will allow you to conceive and develop the next product cycle while your competitors are spending their time playing catch-up.

Doing this enables you to turn threats (of competitive products)

---

31 Jeff Bezos, https:/hbr.org/2020/12/how-amazon-thinks-about-competition, link retrieved 11.01.2022.

into opportunities by figuring out what your customers would prefer instead of the currently available products.

PLAN FOR DOING

Strategy management does not imply analysis-paralysis. You should get enough information, even if the best available information is an assumption. This assumption can then be tested by designing experiments, and you can then act on the new information it reveals. This is a deliberate, concerted effort to create customers and build the team you need to succeed. It is the opposite of crazily throwing everything at the wall and seeing what sticks.

WHAT SUCCESSFUL CEOS DO

As a CEO you have to own your time and priorities. You have to create your agenda and program to achieve your goals, otherwise the demands on your attention will determine where you spend your time. This will inevitably detract from the time you have available to work on your goals.[32]

We have a natural (but often wrong) response to apparent urgent issues. Left unchecked, they will likely contribute to the failure of our business, and/or contribute to us missing valuable opportunities.

> ***The Visible Mission* provides a structured and deliberate approach to help you understand urgency and importance. It will help you to identify and manage both existential threats and opportunities to thrive. It will ensure that you spend your valuable time and energy where they are most needed to achieve your goals.**

32 Michael E. Porter and Nitin Nohria, How CEOs Manage Time, HBR July-August 2019.

As you run your business, there are a thousand things happening that could consume your time and attention. Sometimes a lot of these will pose themselves as urgent issues.

Some of them will be. In some cases, you will be forced to try to restart the engine. But probably fewer times than you imagine.

Some of them will be distracting you from what's important.

You need a way to identify which is which, because in all cases as a CEO, you are required to FLY THE AIRPLANE.

I hope the first three chapters have given you additional motivation to manage more strategically. Now we are ready to take a peek into the more fun, practical stuff.

Part II of *The Visible Mission* starts with the next chapter. There we will dive straight into the practicalities, and you will see that strategy management is easy and clear. It is neither as complicated as rocket science, nor of questionable value like voodoo.

PART TWO

Strategy Management Made Easy: the What and the Why

Maybe you have always wanted to be strategic and to figure out what really makes the most sense for your business. You might wonder if there is an easier way to be strategic, because there is no way you can afford a $2,000/day consultant to do it for you.

If only there was a way that would make strategy easy and accessible, you would embrace it. Something that was real, useful, and not rocket science or voodoo. You would love to be strategic – to lead your team with a vision, knowing what's going on everywhere, having great plans, executing, monitoring, and being able to adjust.

■ CHAPTER 4

Mission Control: Strategy Made Easy

You will probably have seen the pictures and/or video recordings of the Apollo 11 Moon landing, and what NASA's Mission Control Center looked like.

Figure 8 – NASA Mission Control Center during the Apollo Program
Source: https://moon.nasa.gov/resources/184/overall-view-of-mission-operations-control-in-mission-control-center/

The room was bustling, and everyone was there with one purpose: to contribute to the success of the mission. Getting the astronauts to and from the Moon, safely.

This was the first time a living being left the safe confines of the Earth's atmosphere, venturing into space gravity where no food, oxygen (or most of the other conditions that support life) exist.

Imagining and successfully executing this complex effort needed millions of tasks to be coordinated and done by hundreds of thousands of people. That in itself is mind-boggling. It required a unique approach. The Apollo 11 Mission Control Center was created to act as the 'brain' of the operation. All the activities were tracked, the progress was measured, and any mission-related information could be placed in the relevant context to enable the best possible mission execution decisions to be made. It sounds like it was a slow process, but it is better described as a deliberately slow process because the margins for error on a space travel in unimaginably adverse conditions, millions of kilometers from Earth are very, very small. The chances of Apollo 11 exploding were high.

NASA had to have a plan, and they had to execute it and adjust it as mission realities unfolded and demanded.

Imagine walking into a room in your business with your equivalent of NASA's Mission Control Center. There are four large screens, and collectively they show the key details of your entire operation.

The first screen shows your vision and progress.

The second shows both your internal view (what your organization looks like) and your external view (what your business environment looks like).

The third shows your strategic options, choices, and plan to create customers.

The final screen shows your organization in more detail – what you need to succeed, what you have, and your plan for how to close the gap.

This mission control center will be the place where you can place business-related events and developments into context, regardless of whether they are internal to your organization (your plans, your teams, etc.) or external (your business environment, partners, etc.).

This center will be where you will observe, orient, decide and act, like military strategists do.

In the remainder of this book, I will guide you to create your own mission control center. It will enable you to:

- **manage strategically by focusing on your decision options**
- **develop clear plans,**
- **track those plans,**
- **adjust your plans as necessary,**
- **identify real threats and real opportunities faster and earlier, giving you the opportunity to prepare and act appropriately.**

Running an organization is hard: strategy management should not be.

This is a practical book, and I want to apply its key concepts as quickly as possible. Therefore, I now want you to create four landscape pages with the following headings.

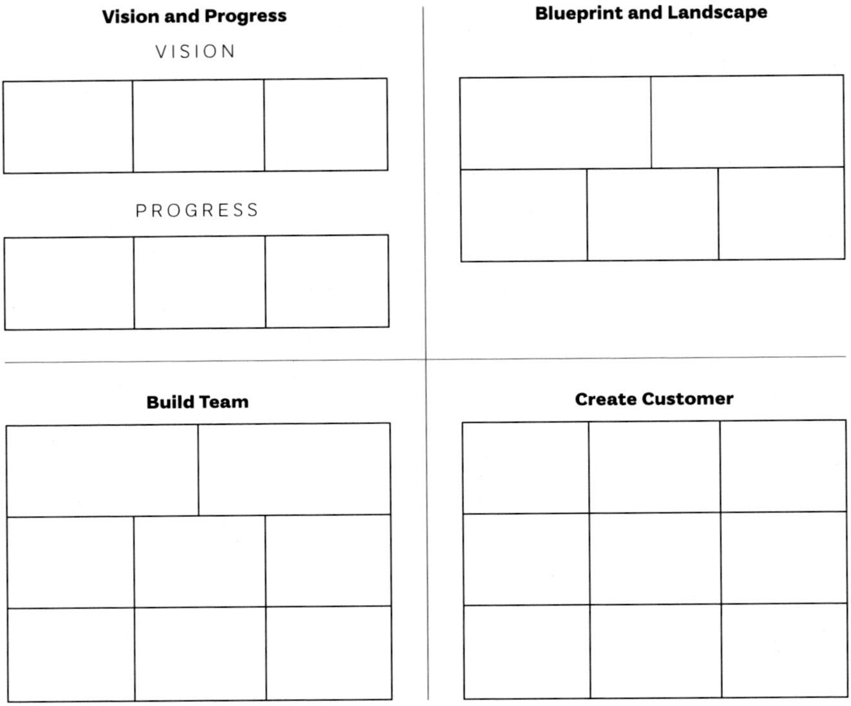

Figure 9 – The four views of the visible mission

We will walk through the details of each of these pages in the coming chapters, capturing what you already have in your business, and guiding you through all the elements that you may need.

The good news is that you will already have some (or maybe even most) of the elements that you will be using to populate and run your mission control center. By the end of Part II of this book, you will likely be able to start using your mission control center to track and steer your business' performance. Even if you don't have everything you need, you will be able to draft these pages and refine them when you do.

The Visible Mission is not about documenting what you have: it's about making the *invisible visible*, and helping you and your team to *clarify and focus on your mission*, as well as *understand your state – internal and external*. It will also help you to *analyze your options*, *develop plans*, *coordinate your efforts*, *track your progress*, and enable *timely, high-quality decisions* as reality unfolds.

Let's look at each of these outcomes in more detail.

- ***Making the invisible visible.***
  Imagine if the Moon landing mission had not had a Mission Control Center where the engineers, physicists, medical experts, etc. could share and coordinate what they knew. Imagine if everyone kept their expertise to themselves or acted in isolation instead. Consider that for the moment. What would have happened to the Moon landing?

  Your organization is unlikely to be as complex as the Apollo Program, but you will likely have a team of people who are working and who know what is going on in their own areas. There will be significant interdependencies, and most likely they are in the heads of individual staff. Unless you make these interdependencies visible, you may not find out about any issues until it is too late.

- ***Clarifying and focusing on your mission.***
  This is the purpose of your organization. It's why your team shows up every day, and why you founded your organization. Do you remember why? Does that reason still inspire you? Does it inspire your team? If it doesn't, you and your team will struggle to make it to your metaphorical Moon and back.

- ***Understanding your state – internal and external.***
  We are going to create a visual guide to your business model. This will get everyone on the same page regarding what you are all doing, and how all the parts fit together. It will improve internal collaboration and coordination in your business. Your external conditions will be similarly visualized, so everyone can

understand the latest information about your industry and your competition, as well as get a rational peek into how the future is shaping up.

- ***Analyzing your options.***
  You will bring your customer insights, market knowledge and access together to decide where to engage with your customers. You will also evaluate the capabilities you need to succeed, check your readiness to do that, and close the gap. This sets your business up for success.

- ***Developing your plans.***
  A mission without a plan is a dream. The plan is a rational approach that breaks the required work down into efforts, or if you use an agile approach, into sprints. The development of the rocket, the capsule, the launch pad, the training of the astronauts, etc. in the Apollo Program would not have been possible without plans.

- ***Coordinating your efforts***.
  Plans and initiatives must not be isolated. Instead, they need to be coordinated between teams, people and resources. The coordination also needs to be ongoing and managed appropriately, especially if its components are ready at different times or they progress at different speeds. For example, the astronauts, launch pad, rocket, capsule, and the support systems all had to be ready at a particular point in the Apollo space program. They were also interdependent, so the interfaces between them had to be coordinated, tested and approved.

- ***Tracking your progress***.
  Of course, your organization's plans and activities must be designed to deliver the agreed goals and the metrics. Without

tracking your progress, you won't know if you have achieved your goals. You may never get anywhere. The astronauts might still be sitting on the launch pad if there was no tracking of the coordinated efforts of all the people working on the Apollo 11 Program. The same is true for the actual flight – where the spacecraft was, and what was supposed to happen at every point needed to be tracked, continuously coordinated, and adjustments made to achieve the ultimate Moon landing goal. No doubt Apollo 11's ground activities also had to be tracked and coordinated through to the mission's successful completion.

- ***Making timely, high-quality decisions***.
  Having all of the above mission control center elements in place helps you to make timely, high-quality decisions. For example, all of the elements and the unfolding reality allowed the Apollo 11 Mission Control team to make decisions when needed, and for the right people to make them. Not everything was important or urgent, and the framework of NASA's Mission Control Center allowed new information to be understood within the overall context. It was also appropriate for different key players to be in control of their areas – the launch manager, the flight manager, the pilots, and the captain of the recovery ship – everyone had to make decisions, but everyone understood the decision-making context. That context was established and managed at the Mission Control Center.

WHAT TO EXPECT

In the next five chapters, we will walk through the structure of your mission control center, and you will be encouraged to collect or draft out the elements of it that you have.

We will start with the 'Vision and Progress' view. We will complete this in two stages: Chapter 5 focuses on the 'Vision' component and Chapter 9 on 'Progress'.

Chapter 6 will focus on developing your 'Blueprint and Landscape' view.

After that we will dive into the 'Create Customer' view in Chapter 7, which will be the core of your strategic options.

Then in Chapter 8 we will look at your 'Build Team' view, evaluating what business capabilities you need to succeed, what you have, and we will plan how to close the gap.

Once your plans are in place, Chapter 9 focuses on steering towards success with what you have developed, and tracking your progress.

DON'T DO IT ALL – AT ONCE

As you have seen, there are four views in the Visible Mission, each with a number of elements.

We will help you compile these views step-by-step, so don't feel that it will overwhelm you.

I recommend that you don't try to do everything at once. (But it would be awesome if you can!)

For most people, it's more realistic to read a chapter or part of a chapter, and then spend another 15-30 minutes a day on one of the elements. Even if you do this only on weekdays, you should have your mission control center set up within a calendar month.

EXAMPLES

The examples I will use to illustrate the development of your visible mission are based on the food truck business shown in the 2014 movie, *Chef*. It is imperfect, and at times I will obviously improvise, imagine, and simply make up stuff to demonstrate a point. (However, it is a good Friday night movie to watch!)

> **You are on your way to develop the mission control center for your organization.**
>
> **It will allow you to focus your team's attention, time and energy on those efforts that will enable you to succeed, while also keeping an eye on potential threats and opportunities.**
>
> **Your mission control center will have four parts: Vision and Progress view, Business Blueprint and Landscape view, Create Customer view, and Build Team view.**

I want you to put your four views that you will sketch out on a wall in your office, or whatever space makes most sense as you continue to populate it with the latest information you have.

I want you to imagine walking your leadership team and your whole team through it, as well as maybe sharing it with a strategic partner or potential investors.

I want you to imagine that you will be as comfortable (and as fluent) managing your strategy, as you are being an engineer, a salesperson, a marketing expert, a software developer (or whatever your passion is!).

Let's dive into this!

In the next chapter we will look at your organization's reason for existence. What is your vision? Your mission? We will look at managing your assumptions and goal cycles – the buckets to turn your vision into reality.

CHAPTER 5

Vision and Progress View: Vision

In a speech in 1962, US president John F. Kennedy said: "We choose to go to the Moon in this decade (..), not because [it is] easy, but because [it is] hard."[33]

This is one of the most exciting visions ever put forward by anyone.

It motivated hundreds of thousands of people working on the Moon landing effort. It inspired the imagination of the United States, as well as the imagination of every person that heard it beyond their boundaries.

When we think of strategy as way to achieve something or to 'get somewhere', then the quote from Lewis Carroll's *Alice in Wonderland* gives us a counter-example:

"Would you tell me, please, which way I ought to go from here?"

"That depends a good deal on where you want to get to," said the Cat.

"I don't much care where—" said Alice.

"Then it doesn't matter which way you go," said the Cat.[34]

Without a goal, you are not going to get anywhere. Successful organizations have focus.[35]

---

33 John. F. Kennedy, https:/spacecenter.org/exhibits-and-experiences/starship-gallery/kennedy-podium/, link retrieved 19.01.2022.

34 Lewis Carroll, https:/www.goodreads.com/quotes/449586-alice-would-you-tell-me-please-which-way-i-ought, link retrieved 19.01.2022.

35 In his book *Hidden Champions of the 21st Century*, Hermann Simon goes into detail about this.

Their focus is enabled by having a goal.

Elite athletes are able to achieve their best because they have goals. I am not an elite athlete by any stretch of the imagination. I had been struggling for years to develop a good workout routine until I realized that I run, cycle and swim as part of my mental and emotional well-being, rather than for some random ideal of completing an ironman competition. Once I realized that, I wrote down what aspects of my life are enabled by living a healthy lifestyle (including regular workouts). My goal was a happy and fulfilled life, and without regular workouts, that goal suffers. (My wife will even tell you that if I don't get a solid workout at least five days a week, I become particularly unpleasant to be around!)

Once I clarified my real and value-based goal, my workouts have become a lot more regular, they feel less oppressive, and I am no longer obsessive when the occasional one is missed.

If you want to achieve something, especially if you need to inspire others to achieve it with you, you need to create a vision. You need to make this vision concrete and use it to create focus, so that you can turn it into action and achievements.

As I shared with you in the previous chapter, imagine walking into your own mission control room. You have four views, and each of the views contains the visualized information you need to observe, orient (contextualize), decide, and act – to deal with threats and with opportunities.

The primary view is the 'Vision and Progress' wall. This is the wall where your moonshot is defined, and where you and your team will track your efforts to make the moonshot a reality.

You are here.

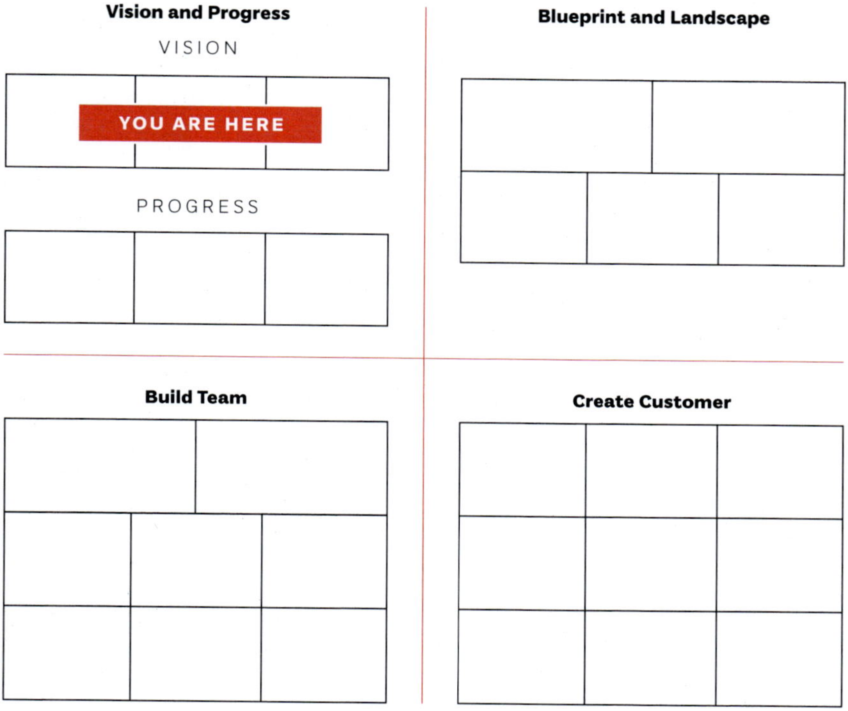

Figure 10 – You are here. There is a 'Vision' worksheet at the end of the chapter (and online at *www.thevisiblemission.com)* for you to use to develop your own visible mission.

The 'Vision and Progress' view consists of two parts: the top 'Vision' part, and the bottom 'Progress' part. As mentioned earlier, we will get to the 'Progress' part Chapter 9 once all of the other elements are in place.

VISION SECTION

The 'Vision' section of the wall is where you describe your:

- vision
- mission,
- goal cycle, and
- assumptions.

Vision and Mission

The first square on the top row of the left-hand side of the 'Vision and Progress' view is where you get to describe your organization's vision and its mission. This is where you define your moonshot. The vision is the description of your future world that you want to help create. This is what you and your team are working on building. The mission describes the 'how' – or more specifically, what you will be doing.

The 'Vision' section of your wall will ultimately help to keep you and your team focused and disciplined. It is the North Star you should base your decisions on when assessing your options.

In the *Chef* movie, head chef Carl's vision is "Touch the lives of people through the experience I give them with the food I cook".[36]

36 Internet Movie Database, https:/www.imdb.com/title/tt2883512/ link retrieved 19.1.2022.

VISION

Touch the lives of people through the experience I give them with the food I cook.

(Carl Casper shares this with Percy, his son, when talking about the quality of the Cuban Sandwich Percy wanted to serve.)

MISSION

Establish a restaurant where I can cook, experiment, and decide, based on my customers and what they enjoy, what goes on the menu.

(After resigning from Gauloise following a disagreement with Riva, the restaurant owner)

Figure 11 – Vision and mission (Chef)

Carl's mission is to 'Establish a restaurant where I can cook, experiment, and decide (based on my customers and what they enjoy) what goes on the menu.

TO DO

NB – This is not optional.

- If you have a document, worksheet or tool where your vision and mission are already defined somewhere (in whatever form), then collect, print or copy it. (Also add the source information – whether it is an app, database or document.)
- If you don't have your mission and vision defined, draft it using the samples shown here – even on an envelope is a good enough start.
- Place your information (or draft) in its assigned space on the top left-hand square of your 'Vision and Mission' view.

Goal Cycle

This is the middle square in the top row of the 'Vision and Progress' view. If the vision and mission describe your moonshot, your goal cycle is where you break it into workable and executable periods. The 'cycle' wording indicates that you will do this work over and over – each time moving you towards your vision.

A goal cycle is a time-bound planning unit. It usually contains a small set of goals, and each goal has metrics so that you can measure your progress towards achieving it. Too many goals diffuse the focus, making it less likely you will succeed.

(It is best practice to have only one active goal cycle. However, it is not unusual to have a number of goal cycles spanning different time horizons. The current, active goal cycle is typically a six-month or year-long horizon. Other typical cycles, which also act as planning vehicles, are an intermediate term with a horizon of two to three years, and a long-term cycle that is typically between five and ten years.)

The goal cycle is a focused effort on achieving a particular result (or set of results). The entire team directs its energy and resources to achieve the goal (or set of goals). The goal cycle is the game plan on how to achieve the goal.

Head chef Carl had a number of early goal cycles – which is not unusual for a start-up business. First to get the truck running and the kitchen working. He named his food truck "El Jefe". Then he wanted to test the kitchen in Miami. After that, they were going head west, cooking their way back to Los Angeles.

GOAL CYCLE
NAME **Food Truck** (Although his ex-wife Inez has been suggesting that he gets a food-truck, it was only after his firing / resignation after the Twitter and social-media flame-out that Carl is left with few other options.)
ASPIRATIONAL GOAL **Get truck and kitchen ready, and tested, and ready to cook.** (He gets the truck from his ex-wife's ex-husband and although it looks like it is dragged ot of a war-zone, Carl, Percy, and Tony fixes it up.)
ASPIRATIONAL DATE / DURATION **A couple of days cleaning, fixing, and replacing old equipment.** (There is no clear deadline, but Carl wants to get it ready as quickly as possible, and establish the line-cooking practice.)

Figure 12 – Goal cycle (El Jefe)

TO DO

- If you have a goal cycle document, worksheet or tool like the one in Figure 12 already defined somewhere (in whatever form), collect, print or copy it. (Add the source information – whether it is an app, database, documentation, or even if it is in a person's head (including your own!).)
- If you don't, sketch it using the sample visualization – on an envelope or sticky note.
- Alternatively, you may choose to assign this task to someone who may be well-positioned to produce or draft your goal cycle – add it to a sticky note, and set up a meeting with the person to explain what you are looking for.

- If you aren't in a position to do any of the above now, add a sticky note with "LATER" on it.
- Place your information, draft or sticky note in the middle square of the top row of your 'Vision and Progress' view.

Assumption Matrix

The square on the right hand-side of the top row of the 'Vision and Progress' view is where you place your assumptions matrix. There are many assumptions within organizations. Many of them are not expressed, and some of them are critical. The assumption matrix provides a location where important assumptions can be collected and shown.

Placing these assumptions in a prominent place on the 'Vision and Progress' view keeps them front and center for everyone. Not only that, it's often possible to test the assumptions, which in turn helps everyone to develop a better grasp on the risks you are facing. This can lead to the development of strategies to help reduce those risks.

With Carl's example, there are three assumptions. The cuisine is critical, but it is not uncertain because Carl knows the food scene, and he has a good grasp on the customers. However, although getting a food truck was obviously very important, the uncertainty surrounding it was much higher. Would it run? Would they be able to clean it well enough? And would they be able to get the kitchen up and running for all they wanted to cook?

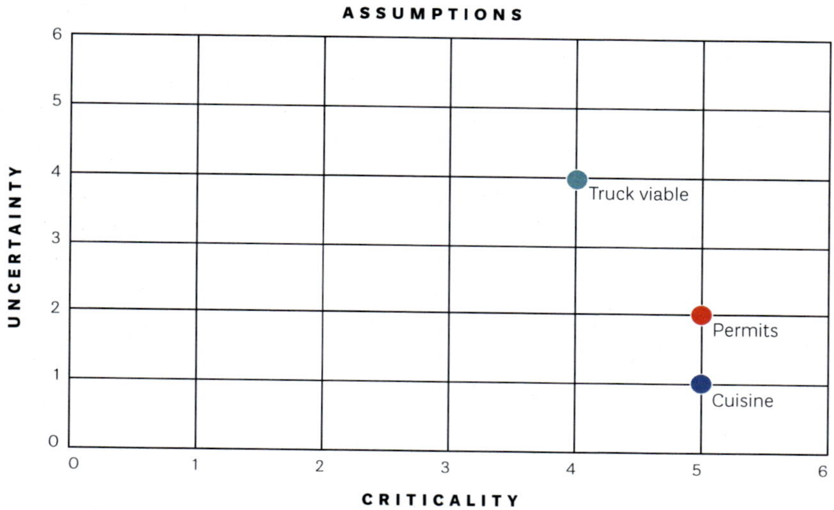

Figure 13 – Assumption matrix (El Jefe)

TO DO

- If you have a document, worksheet or tool like the above assumptions matrix already defined somewhere (in whatever form), collect, print or copy it. (Add the source information – whether it is an app, database, documentation, or even if it is in a person's head (including your own!).)
- If you don't, sketch it using the sample visualization – even on an envelope.
- Alternatively, you may choose to assign this task to someone who may be well-positioned to produce or draft your assumptions matrix – add it to a sticky note, and set up a meeting with the person to explain what you are looking for.
- If you aren't in a position to do any of the above now, add a sticky note with "LATER" on it.
- Place your information, draft or sticky note on the far right square on the top row of your 'Vision and Progress' view.

> **The 'Vision' section describes the purpose of your organization. It is the North Star that will guide your choices and drive your decisions.**
>
> **You will turn your vision into reality through the achievement of a series of goals. The goal cycle will enable you to turn your ideas into actions and achievements.**
>
> **Keeping your assumptions in front of you will keep you honest about what you don't know, and help you know what to test before risking too much.**

John F. Kennedy provided a vision of going to the Moon. The idea not only gripped the world, it inspired and directed the efforts of hundreds of thousands of people, and it ultimately succeeded. Alice didn't care where she was going.

Which of these two scenarios describe your current situation best?

The 'Vision' section of the 'Vision and Progress' view is where you define where you are going. This is the place that you are leading your team towards. Outlining your vision is the first (and a crucial) step that you need to take to get your team and other stakeholders aligned, excited and energized.

Once you have outlined your vision, you and your team know where you are going. But if you plan to travel to your metaphorical Moon, you need to look at your space craft, and to know the environments you have to navigate through.

Your organization does not function in isolation: you exist in a particular time, place and industry. In the next chapter, we will look at developing the 'Blueprint and Landscape' view of your visible mission (your business blueprint and competitive landscape).

'VISION' WORKSHEET

Vision and Mission	Goal Cycle(s)	Assumptions
Who: **YOU**	Who:	Who:
Where: it depends	Where:	Where:
Target Date: **BEFORE YOU CONTINUE**	Target Date:	Target Date:

Note that a digital version of this worksheet can be downloaded from the book's website (www.thevisiblemission.com).

CHAPTER 6

(Business) Blueprint and (Strategic) Landscape View

You need to actively monitor both your organization (to ensure it remains in good working order) and your environment (to see if any changing conditions demand a change in your plans). You may need to make changes to your plans during your journey, and sometimes even change your goal. For example, when an accident caused damage during the 1970 Apollo 13 mission, their Moon landing was abandoned in order to bring the astronauts back to safety.

> **To succeed with your mission, two elements are critical. Firstly, you need the right vehicle. Your organization is your vehicle. Secondly, you need to know your environment to plan your route.**

As you know by now, strategy management is neither rocket science nor voodoo. Let's have a look at where we are in developing your visible mission.

You are here.

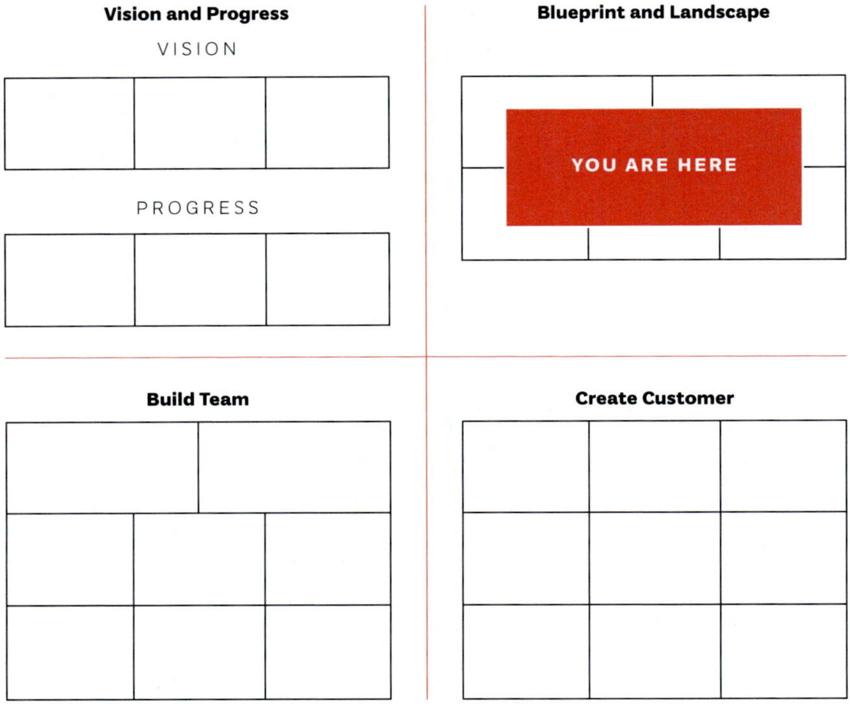

Figure 14 – You are here. There is a 'Blueprint and Landscape' worksheet at the end of the chapter (and online at *www.thevisiblemission.com)* for you to use to develop your own visible mission.

The top row of the 'Blueprint and Landscape' view is your business blueprint section, and the bottom row is your competitive landscape section.

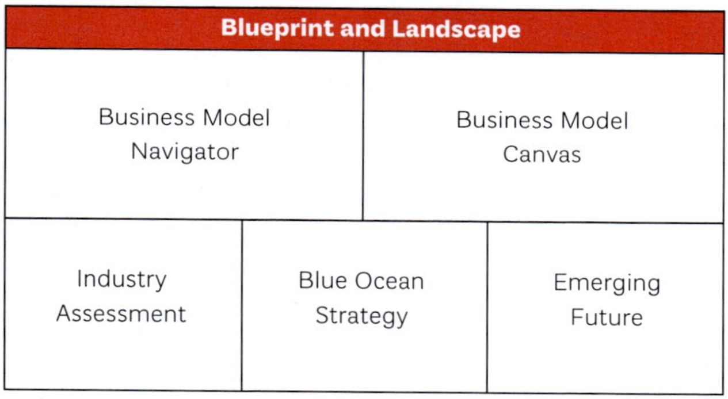

Figure 15 – 'Business Blueprint and Landscape' view

BUSINESS BLUEPRINT SECTION

Think of this section as an x-ray image or an MRI scan of your organization. It has two elements – the first is the Business Model Navigator[37], and the second is the Business Model Canvas.[38] They are related, but they will show different aspects of your business model.

Both are not just great tools to evaluate your opportunities, they are also communication tools you can use with your team, your partners and your stakeholders.

Business Model Navigator

The Business Model Navigator shows the critical outward-looking aspects of your business, as well as your core business model, e.g. digi-

37 Business Model Navigator – Oliver Gassmann, Karolin Frankenberger, Michaela Csik, 2014.

38 Business Model Canvas – Alexander Osterwalder, Yves Pigneur, 2010

tization, platform, etc. It is a great tool to help you consider alternative business models that could potentially fit better within your market.

It also helps you to think through the answers to the critical questions of:

- **who** your customers are,
- **what** you are offering them,
- **how** you are creating your value proposition, and
- **why** your current business model is generating profit for your organization.

In the *Chef* example in Figure 16, we can see this 'who', 'what' 'how' and 'why' information for Carl's business.

Figure 16 – Business Model Navigator (Chef)

TO DO

- If you have a document, worksheet or tool containing the above information already somewhere (in whatever form), collect, print or copy it. (Add the source information – whether it is an app, database, documentation, or even if it is in a person's head (including your own!).)
- If you don't, sketch it using the sample visualization – even on an envelope.
- Alternatively, you may choose to assign this task to someone who may be well-positioned to produce or draft your Business Model Navigator – add it to a sticky note, and set up a meeting with the person to explain what you are looking for.
- If you aren't in a position to do any of the above now, add a sticky note with "LATER" on it.
- Place your information, draft or the sticky note on the left-hand-side of the top row of your 'Blueprint and Landscape' view.

Business Model Canvas

The Business Model Canvas (developed by Alexander Osterwalder and Yves Pigneur) is a great tool to help you understand, visualize and communicate the nine critical business model components. These components include your customer segments, channels, revenues, value proposition, key activities, etc.

You can use the Business Model Canvas to show your team the key components of your business, how they fit together, and what you are doing for your customer segments. In addition, it is a great tool for understanding the implicit interdependencies between the different parts of your organization.

In the *Chef* example in Figure 17, we can see the key business model components identified for head chef Carl's business.

<table>
<tr>
<td rowspan="2" colspan="2">Key Partners

Markets
Farmers
Event organizors
City hall</td>
<td>Key Activities

Options-to-Events
Shopping to Ingredients
Ingredients-to-Menu
Customer-to-Menu
Health-Ready (Cleaning)
Work-to-Play</td>
<td rowspan="2">Product

High quality, affordable, hip food</td>
<td rowspan="2" colspan="2">Value Proposition

Making an event a great experience
Culinary experience</td>
<td>Customer Relations

Personal Assist</td>
<td rowspan="2" colspan="2">Customer Segment

Guests
Event attendees
Event organizor</td>
</tr>
<tr>
<td>Key Resources

Truck
Cooking
Permits
Marketing</td>
<td>Channel

Event Attendance
Truck - branding
Social media
Deliver in person</td>
</tr>
<tr>
<td>Cost</td>
<td>Financial</td>
<td>Item
Food
Staff
Permits
Maintenance</td>
<td>Amount
$ 3,000
$ 2,000
$ 250
$ 300</td>
<td>Item
Sales</td>
<td colspan="2">Amount
$ 15,000</td>
<td>Financial</td>
<td>Revenue & Benefit</td>
</tr>
</table>

Figure 17 – Business Model Canvas (El Jefe)

I use a variation of the original nine-component Business Model Canvas – splitting the original 'Value Proposition' component into 'Value Proposition' and 'Product'.

I do this because in my experience many organizations find it easy to identify their products/services, but more challenging to describe their value propositions. This split breaks those two components apart, and gives you the opportunity to figure out what your value proposition is.

Your product is easier to list because it's the goods you produce and/or the service you provide.

On the other hand, the value that your product provides (or should provide) takes more thought. Not providing value is a major reason why many businesses fail: they introduce products that don't deliver a value proposition to a market and therefore they don't have a viable market.

TO DO

- If you have a document, worksheet or tool like the Business Model Canvas already defined somewhere (in whatever form), collect, print or copy it. (Add the source information – whether it is an app, database, documentation, or even if it is in a person's head (including your own!).)

- If you don't, sketch it using the sample visualization – even on an envelope.
- Alternatively, you may choose to assign this task to someone who may be well-positioned to produce or draft your Business Model Canvas – add it to a sticky note, and set up a meeting with the person to explain what you are looking for.
- If you aren't in a position to do any of the above now, add a sticky note with "LATER" on it.
- Place your information, draft or sticky note on the right-hand side of the top row of your 'Blueprint and Landscape' view.

STRATEGIC LANDSCAPE SECTION

If your business blueprint is like an MRI scan, then your strategic landscape is outward-looking: like a radar or a sonar. It helps you to see what you are surrounded by, and in some cases, what is coming at you!

Your strategic landscape consists of three elements:

1) your industry assessment[39],

2) your emerging future, and

3) your blue ocean strategy.[40]

Let's look at each of these components in more detail.

Industry Assessment

Your industry assessment is a visual overview of the competitive landscape in your particular industry and/or market.

Why is this information important?

---

39 *Competitive Strategy: Techniques for Analyzing Industries and Competitors* by Michael E. Porter, 1998.

40 *Blue Ocean Strategy,* Kim and Mauborgne (2005), Harvard Business Review Press.

It helps you to understand the players in your industry by looking at your:

- customers,
- suppliers (or partners),
- traditional competition,
- new entrants, and
- replacement products.

This information can also help you to decide where to focus your attention to compete more effectively.

Figure 18 is an illustration of head chef Carl's industry assessment for his food truck business. We see that he considers Uber Foods and Lieferando to be replacement products. He is also looking at Rent-a-Chef as a new entrant. (As he was assessing his industry, he might have considered this as another business avenue to explore himself, or perhaps high-end catering.)

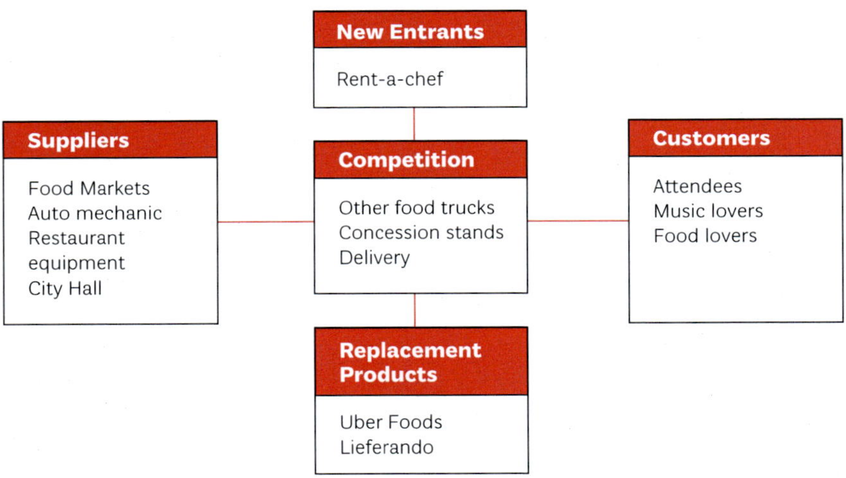

Figure 18 – El Jefe industry assessment (five forces)[41]

41 The 'five forces' tool was developed by Michael Porter.

TO DO

- If you have a document, worksheet or tool like your industry assessment already defined somewhere (in whatever form), collect, print or copy it. (Add the source information – whether it is an app, database, documentation, or even if it is in a person's head (including your own!).)
- If you don't, sketch it using the sample visualization – even on an envelope.
- Alternatively, you may choose to assign this task to someone who may be well-positioned to produce or draft your industry assessment – add it to a sticky note, and set up a meeting with the person to explain what you are looking for.
- If you aren't in a position to do any of the above now, add a sticky note with "LATER" on it.
- Place your information, draft or sticky note on the bottom left-hand square of your 'Blueprint and Landscape' view.

Emerging Future

The industry assessment provides you with a relatively narrow view. That's why we also have an emerging future section for your visible mission. It helps to expand your view and give you a sneak peek into what is coming. It allows you to track major political, environmental, social, technology, legal and economic trends.[42]

I use the term 'emerging future' deliberately since it names the purpose of this tool. It is not intended to be a blind, bureaucratic review: it is intended to track how the future is unfolding, giving you an opportunity to not only prepare for it, but to use it to your advantage.

You can either wait until the future arrives and then react, or you can make use of emerging future information today. While we cannot pre-

---

42 The first letter of each theme forms the acronym "PESTLE".

dict the future, we can see hard trends that are already having an effect on the world. Think climate change, miniaturization, connectivity, etc.

Recall that Netflix asked Blockbuster to be a part of the future. But the Blockbuster people were unable to see what was happening, and they declined Netflix's offer.

Apple has been consistently able to make use of emerging future insights to both prepare itself and lead the way into the future. They were able to bring miniaturization, mobile communication and the internet together in surprising and awesome products, e.g. the iPod, the iPhone and the iPad.

Figure 19 shows some of the trends that Carl has started collecting. Even though he is interested in the regional and seasonal aspects from a food quality perspective, he also knows that this is on the one hand a good marketing approach, especially in Los Angeles. However, he is also considering if there are other options, e.g. get an electric vehicle, instead of the noisy, diesel that he got for free. Maybe something to consider if he makes enough money – it is likely to be a lot less maintenance, and cleaner.

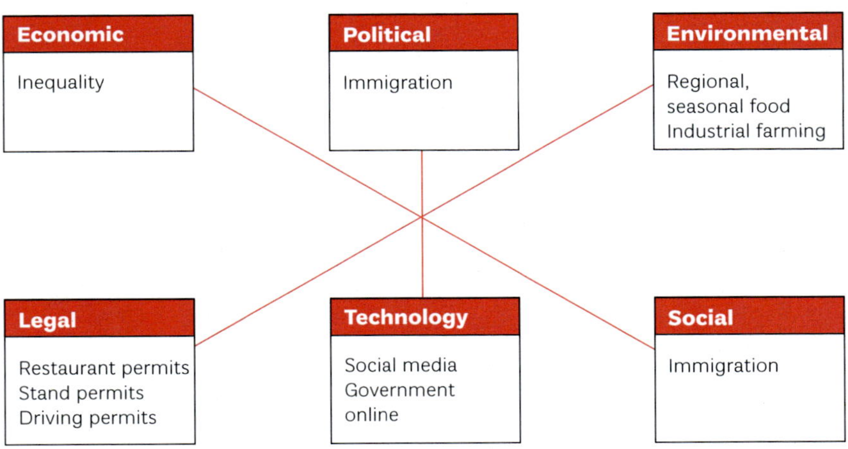

Figure 19 – Emerging future (El Jefe)

TO DO

- If you have a document, worksheet or tool for your emerging future already defined somewhere (in whatever form), collect, print, or copy it. (Add the source information – whether it is an app, database, documentation, or even if it is in a person's head (including your own!).)
- If you don't, sketch it using the sample visualization – even on an envelope.
- Alternatively, you may choose to assign this task to someone who may be well-positioned to produce or draft your emerging future – add it to a sticky note, and set up a meeting with the person to explain what you are looking for.
- If you aren't in a position to do any of the above now, add a sticky note with "LATER" on it.
- Place your information, draft or sticky note on the bottom right-hand square of your 'Blueprint and Landscape' view.

Blue Ocean Strategy

The 'blue ocean strategy' combines the factors important to your customers with your ability to deliver them. In addition, it also allows you to see how well your competitors are measuring up to these factors.

As Kim and Mauborgne describe in their *Blue Ocean Strategy* book, this approach enables you to identify potentially uncontested markets where customers are underserved – the so-called blue ocean market. It is helpful to understand whether you can deliver product or service aspects that your customers are interested in, but which are not currently being addressed by existing options. The blue ocean strategy curve is a visual representation of how your value proposition relates to the factors that are important to your customers. The blue ocean strategy is a great tool to understand and communicate about your customers and your competition.

After doing his blue ocean assessment (see Figure 20), Carl decided that he would really step up the quality of his food – his high-end restaurant experience really set him apart from most other food trucks. When he did his original assessment, he assumed that food truck quality was generally high in his industry. However, after doing some of his own research to test his assumption, he quickly realized that this wasn't the case. With a few exceptions, he discovered that most of his competing food trucks served mediocre-to-low quality food that was expensive. They used lots of supermarket ingredients, processed foods, low quality oils, breads, etc. Carl decided that increasing his food quality would differentiate his El Jefe business and create a competitive advantage.

Figure 20 shows a graphic depiction of Carl's blue ocean strategy for El Jefe. We will explain how this graph was constructed in Chapter 14 when we dig deeper into the 'Blueprint and Landscape' view, helping you to create your own blue ocean strategy.

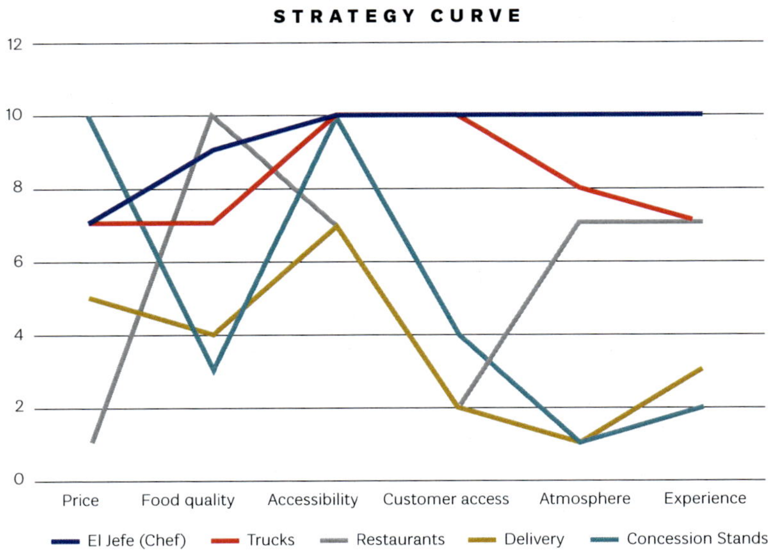

Figure 20 – Blue ocean strategy (El Jefe)

TO DO

- If you have a document, worksheet or tool like the blue ocean strategy already defined somewhere (in whatever form), collect, print or copy it. (Add the source information – whether it is an app, database, documentation, or even if it is in a person's head (including your own!).)
- If you don't, sketch it using the sample visualization – even on an envelope.
- Alternatively, you may choose to assign this task to someone who may be well-positioned to produce or draft your blue ocean strategy – add it to a sticky note, and set up a meeting with the person to explain what you are looking for.
- If you aren't in a position to do any of the above now, add a sticky note with "LATER" on it.
- Place your information, draft or sticky note on the middle square of the bottom row of your 'Blueprint and Landscape' view.

To achieve the vision that is driving you, you need the organization to get you there. Understanding the organization you have today, and knowing what you need for tomorrow is critical: the business model blueprint helps you to identify that key information.

You also need to be able to observe your environment to react in appropriate ways to both the current and evolving reality. The world is constantly changing. To be successful, we all have to be successful today, but we also have to prepare for the future.

The emerging future tools will help you to make the invisible visible, so that you can create a common understanding of your organization and your environment.

The Apollo space program's Mission Control Center tracked both the spacecraft and the environmental conditions to ensure that their various missions succeeded. The success was achieved by actively monitoring what was happening, and being able to make decisions and act when it was necessary. NASA's Mission Control Center adjusted their plans (sometimes radically to ensure that the crew was safe, like during the Apollo 13 mission).

You may not be sending your team into such extreme conditions, however your organization will very likely face existential threats that may put you out of business. The monitoring approach used by NASA will help you and your team reach your goals.

We now have an active blueprint of your organization, and an active map of your industry, your future, and how your product stacks against your competition.

Peter Drucker[43] said that the purpose of a business is to create customers. Without a customer that buys, rents or subscribes to your product or service, your business will cease to exist. In the next chapter we will explore your customer, products, markets and choices.

---

43 *The Practice of Management,* Peter Drucker, 1986.

BLUEPRINT AND LANDSCAPE WORKSHEET

Business Model Navigator	Business Model Canvas
Who: Where: Target Date:	Who: Where: Target Date:

Industry Assessment	Blue Ocean Strategy	Emerging Future
Who: Where: Target Date:	Who: Where: Target Date:	Who: Where: Target Date:

Note that a digital version of this worksheet can be downloaded from the book's website (www.thevisiblemission.com).

CHAPTER 7

Create Customer View

NASA knew what the Apollo space program's vision was – getting humans to the Moon and back. But in order to do that, they needed to solve a series of critical and interdependent challenges:

- getting equipment to space and back;
- getting humans to space and back;
- getting humans into orbit and back;
- getting to the Moon and back; and
- getting humans to the Moon, landed, and back.

All of this needed to be done in a way that dealt with the considerable risk to the people involved and brought it to a manageable and predictable level.

NASA had to work their way up a technological and process ladder, making sure that as little as possible was left to chance, or luck. (In chapter 12 we will look at how they approached this in a little more detail.)

These critical aspects were strategic choices.[44] These issues all had to be addressed and solved one way or another. NASA had to:

---

44 As mentioned in Chapter 1, I use the definition of strategy based on Von Clausewitz. Business is of course not war – his definition of strategy are the choices of engagement with "the enemy". As businesses, our success depends on our choices and the ability to engage with our customers. Rather than conquering our customers, we engage with them to solve their problems. I considered 'customer engagement', but it is an awkward term and settled on 'Create Customer', with a nod to Peter Drucker.

- identify the right issue,
- plan to solve it,
- develop an approach,
- execute the approach, and
- learn from the outcome.

And then repeat this as they take on the next challenge.

As businesses, our strategic challenges involve engaging with our customers:

- how well we understand them and their problems; and
- how well we design, develop, and provide our solutions to solve their problems.

While it's not rocket science, to successfully engage with our customers we need to address a series of challenges that are often interdependent, and they need to be solved one way or another.

In my first job as a programmer, I was responsible for the application that reported the uptime and maintenance windows for the major pieces of equipment (furnaces, etc.) at the steel producer where I worked. My primary customer was Steve, a short, stringy, chain-smoking guy of about sixty. He was friendly but demanding, and I got fed up with his demands for changes, improvements, adjustments to the reports, and how the data was captured. One morning I was complaining loudly about what a terrible customer he was. The senior developer looked at me quietly, waited until I was done, and then said: "Without the customers, you don't have a job."

I remember opening my mouth to respond, but the truth and the meaning behind what she said penetrated my worked-up mind. I closed my mouth, and after a sigh, replied: "Yes, you're right."

Her words still inform how I listen, and what I do today.

Peter Drucker said that the purpose of an organization is to create customers. I think of it a little differently.

One of my professors[45] used to say that we live in a broken and imperfect world.

Our customers find themselves in such a broken and imperfect world. When we help to make their world better and a little less broken by solving some of their problems, then we can succeed. Our organizations exist to understand and meet the needs of these customers, i.e. the people (or other organizations), and through meeting those needs we are given the necessary resources (i.e. we get paid) to continue to survive, and thrive.

The sole purpose of an organization is to create customers.

Your purpose is to understand and empathize with your customers. This understanding will enable you to develop and deliver solutions (products and/or services) that your customers value.

To survive, you need to find the best places to introduce these solutions to your customers.

These efforts are guided by goals, metrics, initiatives and tasks.

These components are brought together in your goal cycles for execution and tracking.

45 I initially studied theology. I have mended my ways since those early days!

You are here.

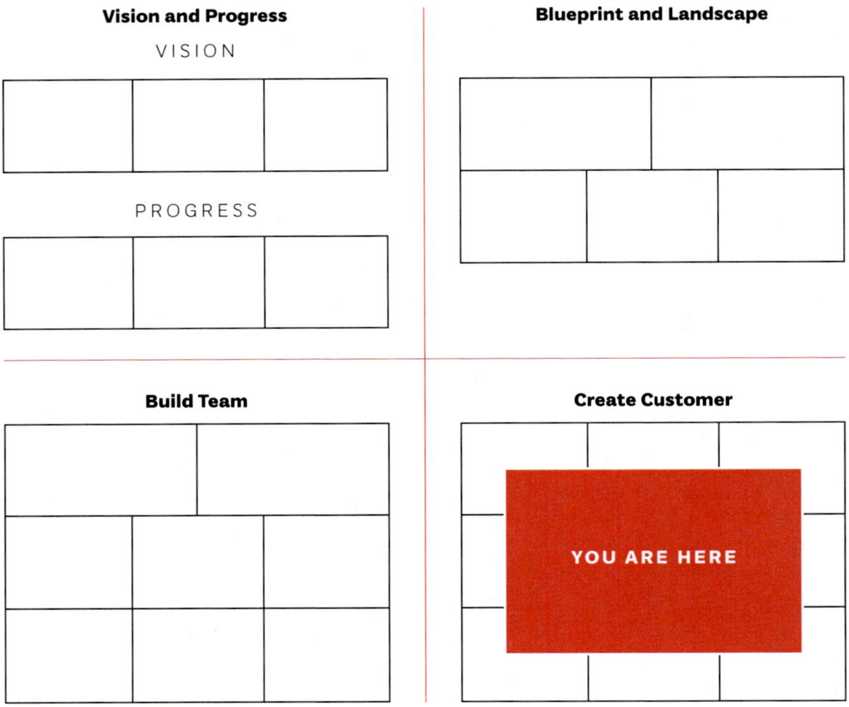

Figure 21 – You are here. There is a 'Create Customer' worksheet at the end of the chapter (and online at www.thevisiblemission.com) for you to use to develop your own visible mission.

The 'Create Customer' view is where we get to describe all of our customer information, or acknowledge where we may have gaps in our knowledge. The view consists of three sections: ***Customer and Product***, ***Market Opportunities***, and finally the ***Goal*** section.

Create Customer			
Customer Empathy Map	Value Proposition	Product	**Customer and Product Section**
Geography	Market Segment	Market Comparison	**Market Opportunity Section**
Goals and Metrics	Roadmap	Costs	**Goal Section**

Figure 22 – 'Create Customer' view

CUSTOMER AND PRODUCT SECTION

The customer and product section has three components:

1) customer empathy map,

2) value proposition, and

3) product.

Let's look at each component in turn in more detail.

Customer Empathy Map

We start with a close view of the customer empathy map. It is no accident that we start with the customer – not the product, not with the value proposition. The customer empathy map is developed around a customer 'persona'. This is an imaginary person with the characteristics that brings the customer to life. Developing the persona makes it easier to relate to the real people it represents.

If we don't understand our customers and the problems they are facing, then we will have difficulty in developing innovative products that they will value. The customer empathy map is a great tool to help you visualize the actions, the mindsets, and the information your customers are dealing with. This in turn will help you to figure out how to help them with our products and services.

Your customer empathy map is a great place to bring together customer insights from your whole team: sales, marketing, product design, user experience, market research, customer support, etc. Together you can build a rich picture of your customers, their concerns, and what they value. Your map can show their pains and gains, and what they hear, see, say, do, think, and feel.

The customer empathy map is also far more 'personal' than the demographic information that you may have used to drive your product development. In some ways, we don't care that much anymore about gender, age, income, etc.

In the following example, we can see how Carl thinks about his customers. He and his team should regularly come back to this map and make sure that it is updated when necessary. This will allow them to identify trends with their customers' behaviors, expectations, etc.

They could of course also look online and monitor what reviews they get, or other social media comments.

WHAT CUSTOMERS **FEEL**	WHAT CUSTOMERS **THINK**
Excited about being at the event	They would like to be able to share about being at his food truck
WHAT CUSTOMERS **HEAR**	WHAT CUSTOMERS **SEE**
Heard about "Le Jefe" food truck	They saw Carl Casper's outburst online They are following him on Twitter They see that he will be at event
WHAT CUSTOMERS **DO**	WHAT CUSTOMERS **SAY**
Attend the event, finf the truck, buy the food Post online Photography themselves at "Le Jefe"	Share with their friends that the food is awesome
CUSTOMER PAINS	**CUSTOMER GAINS**
Hungry at event Food quality often is not so good	Being able to talk about buying at "Le Jefe" Enjoy great food!

Figure 23 – Customer empathy map (El Jefe)

TO DO

- If you have a document, worksheet or tool like the customer empathy map already defined somewhere (in whatever form), collect, print or copy it. (Add the source information – whether it is an app, database, documentation, or even if it is in a person's head (including your own!).)
- If you don't, sketch it using the sample visualization – even on an envelope.
- Alternatively, you may choose to assign this task to someone who may be well-positioned to produce or draft your customer empathy map – add it to a sticky note, and set up a meeting with the person to explain what you are looking for.
- If you aren't in a position to do any of the above now, add a sticky note with "LATER" on it.
- Place your information, draft, or sticky note on the top left-hand square of your 'Create Customer' view.

Value Proposition

The value proposition is a description of how your product meets (or exceeds) the needs of your customers. It does not have to be something that your customers are asking for, but it has to be something that will make their lives better. It will have to lead them out of their broken and imperfect world.

The value proposition is the reality check for you: you need to describe how your product and/or service will solve a particular and critical problem for your customers. It puts you in the shoes of your customers. We almost inevitably fall in love with our own products, but it is our customers who need to value them. Our customers embracing our products/services determine our success, not how much we love our products.

In head chef Carl's value proposition in Figure 24, we can see that the menu products can be adapted to what his customers are likely to value. In his case, great food that is easily accessible. Carl can change his menu based on the region, city, etc.

Value Proposition	Great food experience, brought to where you are.
Customer Segment	Miami pedestrians, park goers.
Pain Reliever	Park visitors might not have packed food - hungry, curious about a new food truck
Gain Creator	Food quality that you did not expect from a food truck. Recognizing the chef that had a meltdown from online videos.

Figure 24 – Value proposition (El Jefe)

TO DO

- If you have a document, worksheet, or tool like a value proposition already defined somewhere (in whatever form), collect, print or copy it. (Add the source information – whether it is an app, database, documentation, or even if it is in a person's head (including your own!).)
- If you don't, sketch it using the sample visualization – even on an envelope.
- Alternatively, you may choose to assign this task to someone who may be well-positioned to produce your draft value proposition – add it to a sticky note, and set up a meeting with the person to explain what you are looking for.
- If you aren't in a position to do any of the above now, add a sticky note with "LATER" on it.
- Place your information, draft or sticky note on the middle square of the top row of the 'Create Customer' view.

Product/Service

This is where you compile everything you need to know about your product/service. How much it will cost you to develop (which informs your pricing), how long it will take, the features, etc. It's important to develop exactly the right product/service that will bring your customers to the place that they want to be, or to an even better place.

We often think that our products are great, but whether our customers value them ultimately determines our success. You need to evaluate your products in relation to your competitor's products and market needs or wants. Some aspects may allow you to charge a premium for your product.

Figure 25 provides an example of the product detail for one of Carl's menu items.

Product	Cuban Sandwiches
Description	Flat bread with ham, mustard, pickles, butter
Price	\$5
Target Date	June 11
Cost	Ham, bread, pickles, mustard, butter Gas, gasoline Permit
Customer Segment	Beach from visitors
Market Size	Estimated 3,000
Market Share	Estimated 10% (300)
Market Value	Revenue \$1,500; tested out the kitchen, equipment, line-cooking process; setting quality standards. Opportunity for marketing.
Assumptions	Food will be valued; Kitchen will function; line-cooking will work well-enough (mostly experienced staff).

Figure 25 – Product detail (El Jefe)

TO DO

- If you have a document, worksheet, or tool that describes your product or service somewhere (in whatever form), collect, print or copy it. (Add the source information – whether it is an app, database, documentation, or even if it is in a person's head (including your own!).)
- If you don't, sketch it using the sample visualization – even on an envelope.
- Alternatively, you may choose to assign this task to someone who may be well-positioned to produce or draft your product/service detail – add it to a sticky note, and set up a meeting with the person to explain what you are looking for.
- If you aren't in a position to do any of the above now, add a sticky note with "LATER" on it.
- Place your information, draft or sticky note on the top right-hand square of your 'Create Customer' view.

MARKET OPPORTUNITY SECTION

The market opportunity section of the 'Create Customer' view will help you to understand whether you have enough customers (or people stuck in a broken and imperfect world) who you can help with your product or service.

This is the core information for your strategic decision-making: identifying existing markets that you can reach with your products and/or services, and your capabilities (e.g., can you produce and distribute to a particular market?). This is where you decide which customers to engage with (i.e. which customers you are going to 'create').

Although it is critical to meet the needs of your customers, it is equally important to know whether there is enough of a (potential) demand for what you will bring. You have to ensure that you have a large enough market to both cover your fixed and operating costs, as well as make a viable profit.

The market opportunity section of the 'Create Customer' view has three components:

1) geography,

2) market segment, and

3) market comparison.

Let's look at each one in turn.

Geography

This component involves describing the accessibility of the geographical regions where we are interested in making our product or service available. It could be a neighborhood, a city, a region, or all the way through to a global presence.

You need to consider your options, including the practicality of both your existing and potential locations where you can and want to serve your customers. This consideration process may help you to identify a series of markets (e.g., local, regional, national, etc.).

Figure 26 provides an example of Carl's customer geography options.

Figure 26 – Customer geography (El Jefe)

TO DO

- If you have a document, worksheet or tool like the one outlined above already defined somewhere (in whatever form), collect, print or copy it. (Add the source information – whether it is an app, database, documentation, or even if it is in a person's head (including your own!).)
- If you don't, sketch it using the sample visualization – even on an envelope.
- Alternatively, you may choose to assign this task to someone who may be well-positioned to produce or draft your customer geography options – add it to a sticky note, and set up a meeting with the person to explain what you are looking for.
- If you aren't in a position to do any of the above now, add a sticky note with "LATER" on it.
- Place your information, draft or sticky note on the left-hand square of the middle row of the 'Create Customer' view.

Market Segment

When you combine your customer segment (that you have described in your customer empathy map) with geography, you build a clear picture of your opportunities.

Your customer segment value is the primary lens through which you can compare different market opportunities, and decide where you want to engage, and where you don't. It will help you look at the pros/cons of your opportunities.

Figure 27 shows a segment for El Jefe, and how it could be evaluated.

Segment	Couples - Miami
Description	Couples attending the beach (park)
Product	High quality food from a food truck
Price	$20 per couple spent on average
Market Size	Event attendees (6.000)
Market Share	600
Number of customers	600 (couples) per day (6 hours)
Cost	$400
Cost Notes	Produce, labor, consumables
Assumptions	Accessibility of local, regional produce and products. $20 spent is based on the price of the items, and what people typically like.

Figure 27 – Customer segment (El Jefe)

TO DO

- If you have a document, worksheet, or tool like this already defined somewhere (in whatever form), collect, print, or copy it. (Add the source information – whether it is an app, database, documentation, or even if it is in a person's head (including your own!).)
- If not, sketch it using the sample visualization – on an envelope.
- Alternatively, you may choose to assign this as a task to someone who may be well-positioned to produce or draft your market segment information – add it to a sticky note, and set up a meeting with the person to explain what you are looking for.
- If you aren't in a position to do any of the above now, add a sticky note with "LATER" on it.
- Place your information, draft or sticky note on the middle square of the middle row of the 'Create Customer' view.

Market Comparison

For each of your considered markets, you will create goals, metrics, initiatives and tasks. This information will enable you to understand the investment needed to develop your identified markets. Determining the investment required and the value of each market will then enable you to compare your options and identify the best opportunity (or opportunities).

In Carl's example, we can see that his 'couples' market segment (the bars on the left in Figure 28) are far more profitable for him than his 'families' market segment. And if he had to choose between cities, New Orleans and Austin are the most profitable. (See the Profit bar – both come in at $19,800 in the 'couples' segment.)

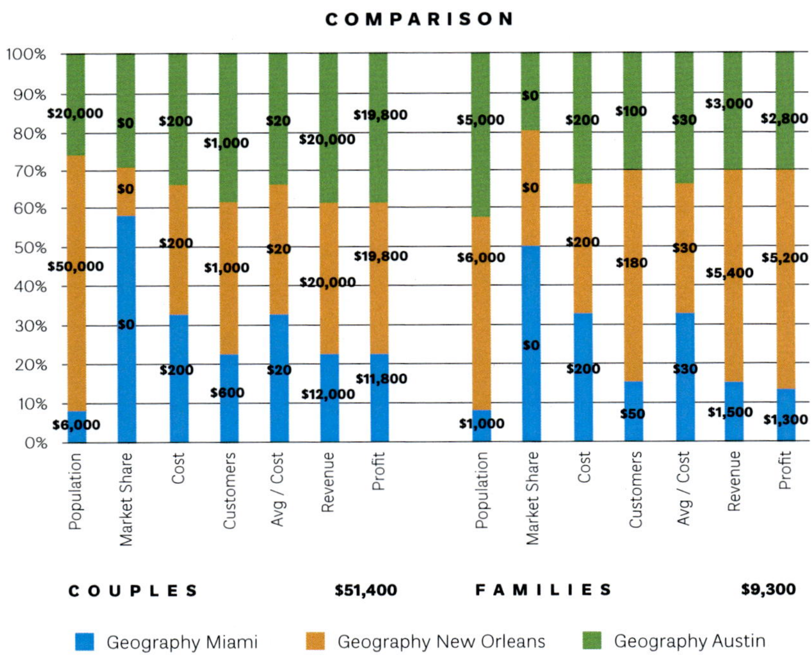

Figure 28 – Example of market comparison (El Jefe)

TO DO

- If you have a document, worksheet or tool that contains your market comparison information (in whatever form), collect, print or copy it. (Add the source information – whether it is an app, database, documentation, or even if it is in a person's head (including your own!).)
- If you don't, sketch it using the sample visualization – even on an envelope.
- Alternatively, you may choose to assign this task to someone who may be well-positioned to produce or draft your market comparison information – add it to a sticky note, and set up a meeting with the person to explain what you are looking for.
- If you aren't in a position to do any of the above now, add a sticky note with "LATER" on it.
- Place your information, draft or sticky note on the right-hand square of the middle row of the 'Create Customer' view.

GOAL SECTION

The goal section of the 'Create Customer' view has three components:

1) goals and metrics,

2) roadmap, and

3) cost.

Goals, Metrics and Initiatives

This is where you will define and look at your options in terms of market size and profitability. One or multiple goals will be selected and shown to set the expectations for what is to be achieved during your goal cycle.[46]

---

46 Goals that you might set in the 'Build Team' view may contribute to your 'Create Customer' goals. (See Chapter 8).

In our fictional example in Figure 29, we see that Café du Monde came in at 120% of its estimated revenue (the orange 'measure' bar), effort was lower than planned, and the cost was a little more.

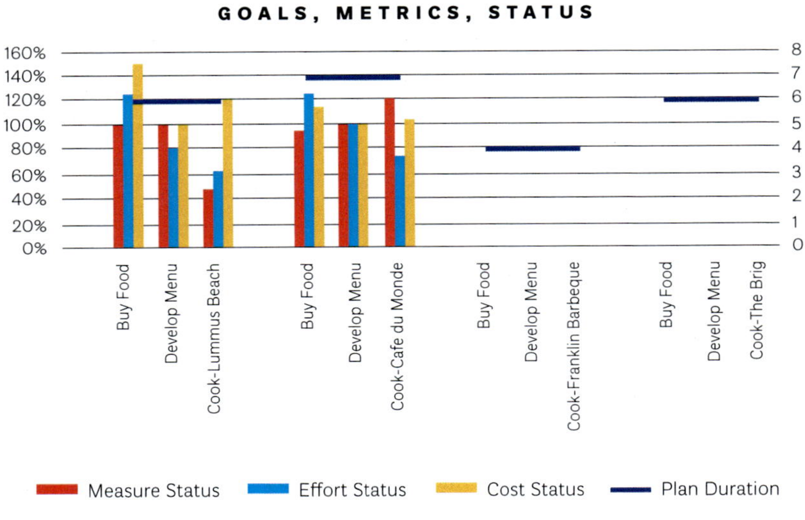

Figure 29 – Goals and metrics (days on right axis) (El Jefe)

TO DO

- If you have a document, worksheet, or tool containing your goals and metrics information somewhere (in whatever form), collect, print or copy it. (Add the source information – whether it is an app, database, documentation, or even if it is in a person's head (including your own!).)
- If you don't, sketch it using the sample visualization – even on an envelope.
- Alternatively, you may choose to assign this task to someone who may be well-positioned to produce or draft your goals and metrics information – add it to a sticky note, and set up a meeting with the person to explain what you are looking for.

- If you aren't in a position to do any of the above now, add a sticky note with "LATER" on it.
- Place your information, draft, or sticky note on the bottom left-hand square of your 'Create Customer' view.

Cost

To achieve your goals, you obviously need resources: people, tools, suppliers, raw materials, etc. Resources cost money. The cost screen will help you and your team to visualize that reality and assess the costs of your initiatives in relation to their value to your organization. It will also make it easier for you to plan and ensure that you have the necessary resources (both financial and non-financial) to achieve your goals. This information is also important when you need to secure investments, loans, etc. to enable you to develop a particular product and/or market.

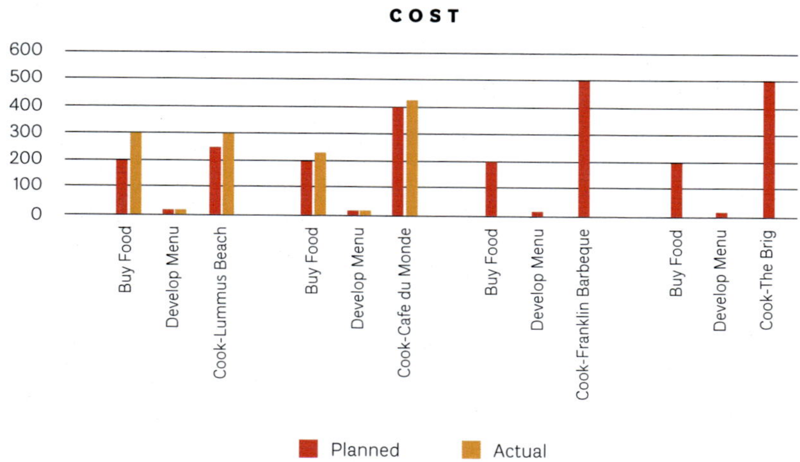

Figure 30 – Initiative costs (El Jefe)

TO DO

- If you have a document, worksheet or tool that contains your cost information somewhere (in whatever form), collect, print or copy it. (Add the source information – whether it is an app, database, documentation, or even if it is in a person's head (including your own!).)
- If you don't, sketch it using the sample visualization – even on an envelope.
- Alternatively, you may choose to assign this task to someone who may be well-positioned to produce or draft your cost information – add it to a sticky note, and set up a meeting with the person to explain what you are looking for.
- If you aren't in a position to do any of the above now, add a sticky note with "LATER" on it.
- Place the information, draft or sticky note on the middle square of the bottom row of your 'Create Customer' view.

Roadmap

The roadmap provides you with your time aspect. It will show you when you are expecting to start, measure and complete your initiatives to achieve your goals. It is a visual calendar view and a great tool to use to:

- get everyone in your organization on the same page,
- consider how the different parts and initiatives need to be coordinated and sequenced,
- track the speed of your progress, and
- monitor your resources.

In Carl's example, since he is traveling in his food truck he allows himself time to get to his destinations, then buy the food he needs, develop his menu, and then attend the planned event.

Goals	Metrics	Date		Plan Duration	1.6	2.6	3.6	4.6	5.6	6.6	7.6	8.6	9.6	10.6	11.6	12.6	13.6	14.6	15.6	16.6
		Start	Target																	
TEST COOKING		06.06.14	11.06.14																	
	Buy Food	06.06.14	11.06.14	6																
	Develop Menu	06.06.14	11.06.14	6																
	Cook - Lummus Beach	06.06.14	11.06.14	6																
NEW ORLEANS		13.06.14	18.06.14																	
	Buy Food	13.06.14	18.06.14	7																
	Develop Menu	13.06.14	18.06.14	7																
	Cook - Cafe du Monde	13.06.14	18.06.14	7																

Figure 31 – 'Create Customer' roadmap (El Jefe)

TO DO

- If you have a document, worksheet or tool like the roadmap already defined somewhere (in whatever form), collect, print or copy it. (Add the source information – whether it is an app, database, documentation, or even if it is in a person's head (including your own!).)
- If you don't, sketch it using the sample visualization – even on an envelope.
- Alternatively, you may choose to assign this task to someone who may be well-positioned to produce or draft your roadmap – add it to a sticky note, and set up a meeting with the person to explain what you are looking for.
- If you aren't in a position to do any of the above now, add a sticky note with "LATER" on it.

- Place your information, draft or sticky note on the bottom right-hand square of the 'Create Customer' view.

Your goals, metrics, initiatives and tasks will form the basis for monitoring your progress (the bottom row of the 'Vision and Progress' view). Since you may also have some initiatives you need to develop to improve your organization's capabilities, we will combine your 'Create Customer' initiatives (those that generate revenue for your business) with your 'Build Team' initiatives (the capabilities to execute your revenue-generating initiatives – more about these in the next chapter).

The key aspect of strategy is deciding which customers that you could and should be engaging with, and how you should be bringing valuable solutions to their problems.

Without knowing, understanding and empathizing with your customers, you will be very unlikely to meet their needs. Instead, you will largely be depending on luck to excite them with your creative and innovative solutions.

A market evaluation will help you to figure out how to make your business viable, and enable you to survive and thrive.

The plan you develop brings the solution(s) to your customer through your initiatives and tasks that are set up to achieve your defined goals and metrics. You succeed when your customers reward you by paying for the solutions you provide.

NASA was able to identify which series of technological and managerial issues they needed to address, and how to solve them. Solving their way up the metaphorical ladder enabled them to solve the entire challenge of the Moon landing, one mission at a time. Each mission used the experience, information, organization and equipment developed during the previous one.

Steve (my chain-smoking customer in my first job as a programmer) did me an amazing favor. He came to me and told me what he wanted. It is a gift when our customers share with us how their world is imperfect and broken, and ask us to help them make it better.

I have learned to truly care about my customers, and to pay attention to their needs. Our customers don't always know the best way to solve their problems. That's where we come in. When we understand their problems, we can come up with innovative and creative solutions.

If you want to succeed in understanding your customers, you need to build the right products/services for them. In order to develop customer insights to inform your product development, you also need an organization with the right abilities. In the next chapter, we will look at how we develop such an organization by developing the right team capabilities.

'CREATE CUSTOMER' WORKSHEET

Customer Empathy Map	Value Proposition	Product
Who: Where: Target Date:	Who: Where: Target Date:	Who: Where: Target Date:
Geography	**Customer Segment**	**Market Comparison**
Who: Where: Target Date:	Who: Where: Target Date:	Who: Where: Target Date:
Goal and Metrics	**Roadmap**	**Cost**
Who: Where: Target Date:	Who: Where: Target Date:	Who: Where: Target Date:

Note that a digital version of this worksheet can be downloaded from the book's website (www.thevisiblemission.com).

CHAPTER 8

Build Team View

NASA obviously needed an organization to make all their missions work to achieve the 1969 Moon landing. NASA was established in 1958. It needed people, processes, information, tools and technologies. These organizational capabilities had to be assembled and developed as things happened. Let's look at each capability in turn.

- **People**
  NASA needed physicists, engineers, spacecraft builders, etc. Its people were developed individually and as teams through training, and it became an organization with a common purpose.
- **Processes**
  NASA needed processes to analyze, design, prototype, build, test, manage, learn, communicate, etc.
- **Information**
  NASA needed information to understand and apply the physics, as well as information to communicate and coordinate all of its activities.
- **Tools and technologies**
  NASA needed tools and technologies, and in many cases, the tools and technologies had to be designed and built from scratch. They needed technologies to manage vast amounts of data.

All of these capabilities needed to be interrelated and developed as they were needed to enable NASA astronauts to both land on the Moon and get back to Earth safely.

For you to succeed with your customer creation goals, you either need to have the capabilities your organization needs in place, or you need to develop them to be ready in time.

Let me tell you a story.

Growing up in South Africa was interesting for me, and not least because television was only introduced there in 1975. I consider growing up with the radio an unusual privilege.[47]

Around the age of 10, I was listening to the radio in our living room and heard Beethoven's fifth symphony for the first time. The passion and power of the music made it impossible for my 10-year-old self to sit still – I jumped up and conducted my imaginary orchestra.

Beethoven broke the mold of many composition forms, including the symphony.[48] In addition, his symphonies demanded different things from the orchestra. The orchestra had to change to accomplish the experience he wanted to share with his audience. Beethoven shaped the orchestras and their performance to fit his music and the experience he wanted to share with the audience.

In the same way, it is your responsibility and opportunity to shape your organizational team around what you are intending to share with your 'audience' – your customers.

You need a team to deliver your vision with you. You are responsible for finding, involving, inspiring, developing and engaging your team.

It is not only people you need to build your team. For them to perform, you need the right processes, information, tools and technologies.

---

47 I also a little guiltily subscribe to Steve Allen's quote: "Radio is the theater of the mind; television is the theater of the mindless."

48 *Harvard Dictionary of Music,* Don Michael Randel, 2003.

You are here.

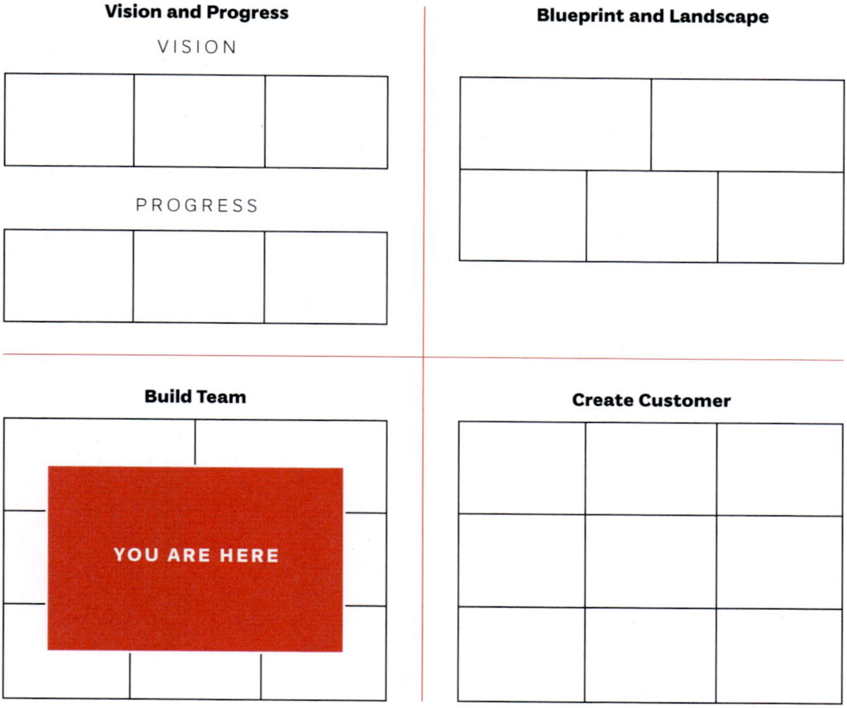

Figure 32 – You are here. There is a 'Build Team' worksheet at the end of the chapter (and online at www.thevisiblemission.com) for you to use to develop your own visible mission.

The 'Team Build' view helps you to build the right team to do the work needed to achieve your goals. You are not only building your team for your current set of goals and metrics, you are building your team and your organization for your next goal cycle as well. And the cycle after that. The idea is that you will build your organization in such a way that you can take on different goals, and explore different customer creation options. If your 'Create Customer' view is the core of your strategic decisions, then your 'Build Team' view is the core of how you execute your strategies.[49]

During the completion of your Business Model Canvas in Chapter 6, we started looking at some of the elements critical to your ability to succeed: your key activities and your key resources.

---

49 Von Clausewitz (from a military context) refers to 'executing strategies' as 'tactics'. Tactics are also a combination of people, process, tools and technologies, and information – all applied to achieve a particular outcome in service of the strategy.

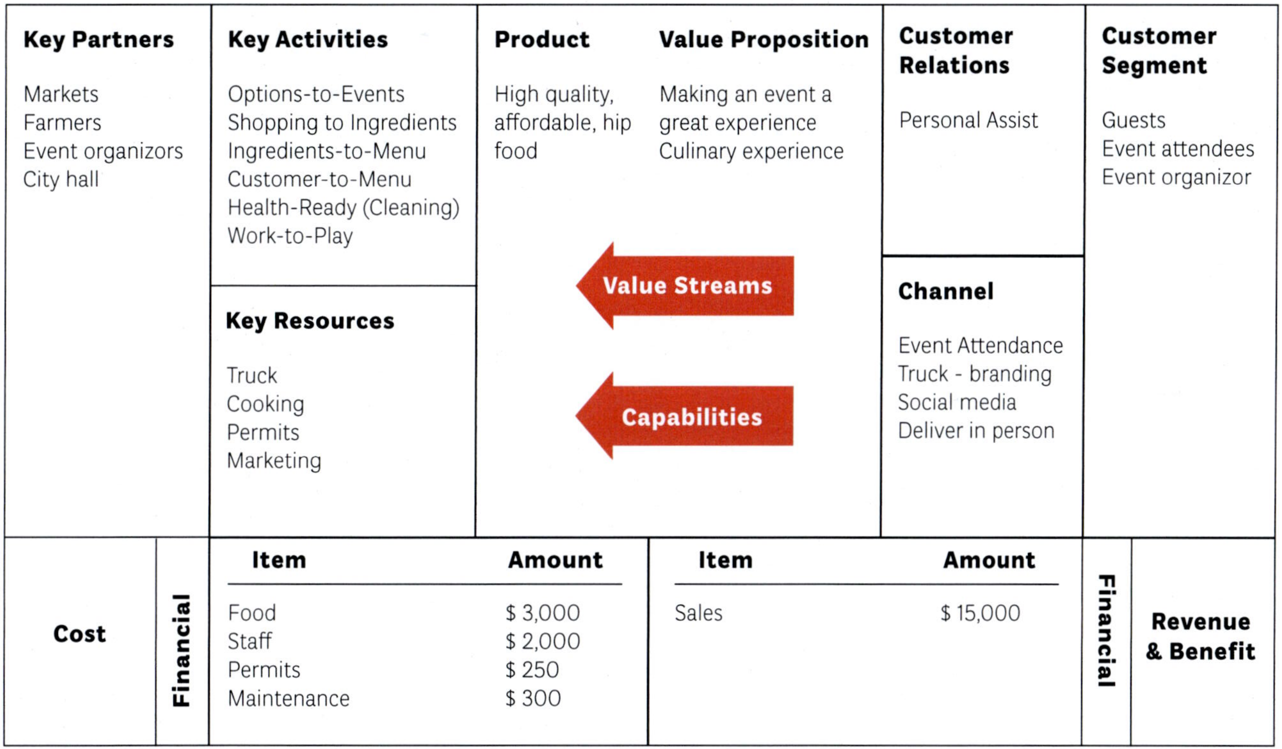

Figure 33 – Business Model Canvas (El Jefe)

As I mentioned in Chapter 6, your key resources are best understood as being your capabilities, and your key activities are best understood as being the value streams those activities create.[50] But if you want to stick to the terms 'key resources' and 'key activities', that's fine. The main thing is to use the practices behind them. You will see in a moment why I use the 'key resources' and 'key activities' terminology.

KEY RESOURCES (CAPABILITIES)

Key resources are often shown individually, but are better described when packaged as a capability. Your people, processes, information, tools and technologies are all resources, but they function as a capability. For example, product management, project management, product development, human resource management, etc.

A capability is the ability to deliver an outcome relevant to your business. The capability is ensured through the right combination of people, processes, information, tools and technologies. Each capability must be focused on meeting your desired result.[51]

Capabilities are often expressed as systems – e.g. a CRM system (customer relationship management), project management tools, etc. It is useful to identify these systems, since it allows you to discover whether the same 'problem' is resolved multiple times throughout your organization. More about this in Chapter 16.

Sometimes capabilities are expressed as organizational units – e.g. HR, IT, etc. There is nothing wrong with that, as long as you don't confuse organizational systems with organizational units. You can implement a capability through a dedicated organizational unit. Or you may

---

50 In his 2004 Ph.D. thesis *The Business Model Ontology: A Proposition in a Design Science Approach,* Alexander Osterwalder actually calls a set of resources a capability. The 'key activity' was originally a 'value configuration'.

51 Adapted from *The Essential Advantage,* Leinwand and Mainardi, Harvard Business Review Press, 2010.

choose to have a single capability handled by multiple parts of your organization. For example, product management typically spans research and design teams, product development, manufacturing engineers, warehouse management, etc.

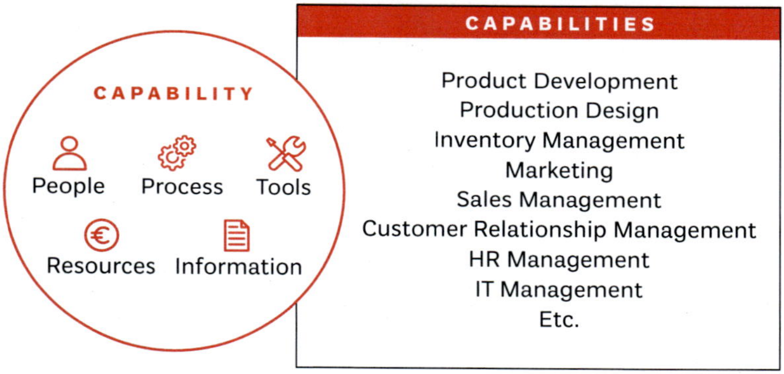

Figure 34 – Capabilities: people, processes, information, tools and technologies

If you think of your capabilities as key resources, then you can imagine them as a toolbox of things you can do.

But what is it that you want to do? How do you use and apply your key resources (capabilities)?

In the 'Create Customer' view, we said that to create customers you must deliver something of value to them. This activity of delivering value is what we call the 'value stream'.

KEY ACTIVITIES (VALUE STREAMS)

A value stream is a sequence of activities that your organization undertakes to deliver on a customer request.[52] You have value streams at your organization, whether you call them by that name or not. A value

52 *Value Stream Mapping*, Martin and Osterling, McGraw Hill, 2013.

stream is an end-to-end process[53] with a starting point through to delivery (e.g. order-to-cash, recruit-to-employment, hire-to-retire, concept-to-design, design-to-manufacture, etc.) A value stream is therefore a set of activities (using a combination of capabilities) to produce a particular value for customers. (Customers could be external to your organization, or internal – e.g. your marketing department, etc.)

Let's look at an order-to-cash value stream. It is initiated by a customer's order, and finishes when we receive the customer's payment, and when she/he has received the desired product/service.

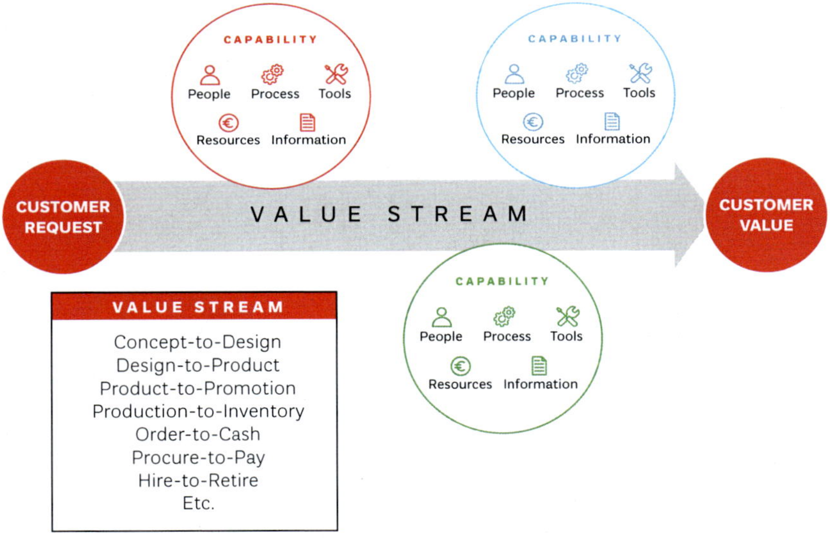

Figure 35 – Value stream (process) mock-up

In your 'Build Team' view, you are going to look at what value streams you have. You will compare the current state of your value streams with your desired state, so you can determine the gap. Your 'Build Team' goals and plans will then close this gap by developing

53 Although not calling it the 'value stream' by name, *Reengineering the Corporation* (Hammer and Champy, 2006) is one of the seminal works about the concept.

the right value streams to the necessary level to achieve your 'Create Customer' goals.

Figure 36 is a representation of what capabilities and value streams usually look like in organizations. This representation presents all kinds of challenges, as well as opportunities to turn an organization into a formidable player.

If you don't have all of your capabilities and resources defined at the moment, don't worry. You will get a chance to draft them out later. An approach is shared in Chapter 16.

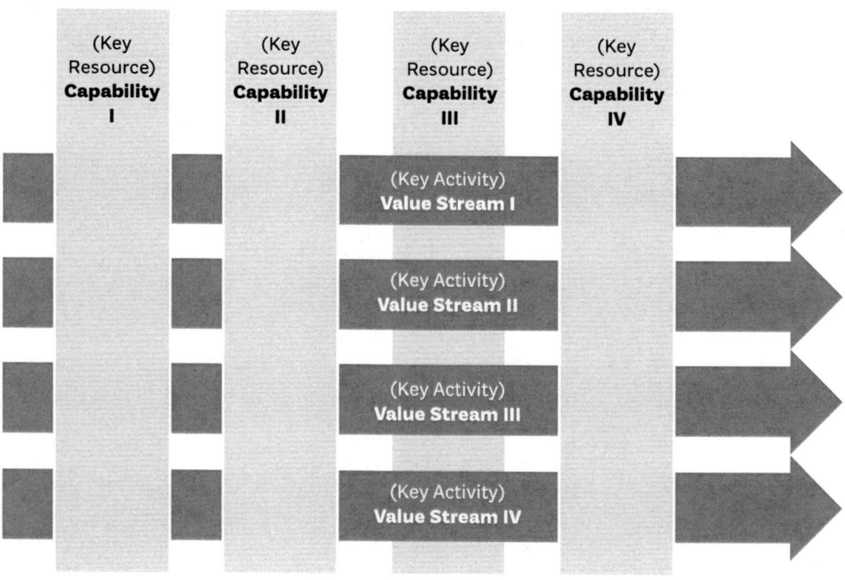

Figure 36 – Value streams and capabilities

Your 'Build Team' view consists of three sections: your '**Value Stream'** section, your '**Assessment**' section, and your '**Goal'** section. Let's look at each section in turn.

<table>
<tr><th colspan="6">Build Team</th><th></th></tr>
<tr><td colspan="3">Capabilities
(Key Resources)</td><td colspan="3">Value Streams
(Key Activities)</td><td>Value Stream Section</td></tr>
<tr><td colspan="2">Value Stream Analysis</td><td colspan="2">Assessment Matrix</td><td colspan="2">Urgency</td><td>Assessment Section</td></tr>
<tr><td colspan="2">Goals and Metrics</td><td colspan="2">Roadmap</td><td colspan="2">Costs</td><td>Goals Section</td></tr>
</table>

Figure 37 – 'Build Team' view

VALUE STREAM SECTION

This section has two components – your capabilities (key resources) and your value streams (key activities). Let's look at the 'Capabilities' component first. As we have seen earlier, a capability is your ability to deliver an outcome relevant to your business. It is a combination of people, processes, information, tools and technologies – all focused on meeting the desired result.

Capabilities (Key Resource / Functions)	Responsible
Cooking	All
Money Management	Carl
Inventory	Tony
Permit Application	Carl
Marketing	Percy
Truck Signage	Percy
Truck Maintenance	Tony
Purchases	Carl

Figure 38 – El Jefe's capabilities (key resources)

TO DO

- If you have a document, worksheet, or tool that already defines your organization's capabilities somewhere (in whatever form), collect, print or copy it. (Add the source information – whether it is an app, database, documentation, or even if it is in a person's head (including your own!).)
- If you don't, sketch it using the sample visualization – even on an envelope.
- Alternatively, you may choose to assign this task to someone who may be well-positioned to produce or draft your organization's capabilities – add it to a sticky note, and set up a meeting with the person to explain what you are looking for.
- If you aren't in a position to do any of the above now, add a sticky note with "LATER" on it.
- Place your information, draft or sticky note on the left-hand side of the top row of your 'Build Team' view.

Now let's look at the other component of the value stream section of your visible mission – your value streams. Figure 39 lists the value streams for chef Carl's El Jefe business.

Ingredients-to-menu is an example of one of his value streams. This value stream required Carl to develop a menu for his food truck based on what ingredients he could source at the local markets. To create a value stream, those ingredients needed to be combined with his experience and skill in imagining and creating food that will ultimately please his customers. Carl does not buy ingredients that will sacrifice the quality of his food. He also does not try to force his menu on his shopping activity by trying to buy ingredients that are out of season or that are non-regional products. Although he doesn't throw money away, he also doesn't sacrifice food quality in favor of cost. He effectively brings his ingredients, experience, cooking knowledge, and knowledge of what people enjoy together in a successful process. Ultimately, he delivers a menu that excites and pleases his customers. That's a value stream.

EL JEFE		
Value Streams	**Responsible**	**Deliverable**
Options-to-Events	Carl	Great Events
Shopping-to-Ingredients	Carl	High quality ingredients
Ingredient-to-Menu	Carl	Exciting menu options
Event-to-Awareness	Tony	Excited customers
Event-to-Permit	Carl	Permission to sell
Work-to-Pay	Carl	Content Employees
Budget-to-Actual	Tony	Well managed finances
Customer-to-Meal	Carl	Delighted customers
Health-Ready (cleaning)	Tony	Healthy customers
Bill-to-Paid	Carl	Supportive vendors
Use-to-Run (Maint.)	Tony	Ability to attend events

Figure 39 – El Jefe's value streams (key activities)

TO DO

- If you have a document, worksheet or tool that contains your value stream information already defined somewhere (in whatever form), collect, print or copy it. (Add the source information – whether it is an app, database, documentation, or even if it is in a person's head (including your own!).)
- If you don't, sketch it using the sample visualization – even on an envelope.
- Alternatively, you may choose to assign this task to someone who may be well-positioned to produce or draft your value streams - add it to a sticky note, and set up a meeting with the person to explain what you are looking for.
- If you aren't in a position to do any of the above now, add a sticky note with "LATER" on it.
- Place your information, draft or sticky note on the left-hand side of the top row of your 'Build Team' view.

ASSESSMENT SECTION

The assessment section of the 'Build Team' view helps you to discover exactly what you need in terms of your capabilities and value streams.

Here you identify which 'league you need to be playing in' to succeed with your 'Create Customer' goals. Then you need to figure out which 'league' you are actually playing in right now. The gap between these will be closed by defining your 'Build Team' goals and metrics. These goals will be achieved through your initiatives.

An effective assessment should allow you to prioritize your value streams in terms of your 'Create Customer' goals. If you don't know which of your value streams are the most important, you run the risk of focusing your attention on those that are less important. You also need to evaluate the readiness of your value streams to achieve your goals.

The assessment section of the 'Build Team' view has three components:

1) value stream analysis,

2) an assessment matrix, and

3) urgency.

Let's look at each component in turn.

Value Stream Analysis

This section of the 'Build Team' view will show you the detail of each of your value streams, including its relative priority, its current maturity level, its required maturity level, and what needs to be done to bridge any maturity level gaps.

Figure 40 shows a value stream analysis for the 'shopping-to-ingredients value stream for chef Carl's El Jefe business.

Value Stream	Shopping-to-Ingredients
Description	Shopping for local, seasonal ingredients to base the menu on.
Deliverable	High quality produce and ingredients to form the basis for the event menu.
Priority	5 - This is a critical aspect of the quality of food produced.
Current Readiness	5 - Excellent. Based on restaurant experience.
Future Readiness	5 - stays as it is, adjust to location, etc.
Integration	Shopping is influenced by the event, type of event. It also sets the base for thecooking menu.
Standardization	No integration applicable, outside the expense management.
Cost	$400 total ($300 (produce), $80 (time), $20 (travel)).
Cost Notes	Cost of produce, equipment. Cost of time doing the shopping. 2 hours each for Carl and Tony at $40/hour.
Assumptions	Accessibility of local, regional produce and products.
Recommendation	Work to retain the standard; consider training John, and taking Percy along.

Figure 40 – Value stream analysis for El Jefe

TO DO

- If you have a document, worksheet or tool that contains your value stream analysis somewhere (in whatever form), collect, print or copy it. (Add the source information – whether it is an app, database, documentation, or even if it is in a person's head (including your own!).)
- If you don't, sketch it using the sample visualization – even on an envelope.
- Alternatively, you may choose to assign this task to someone who may be well-positioned to produce or draft your value stream analysis – add it to a sticky note, and set up a meeting with the person to explain what you are looking for.
- If you aren't in a position to do any of the above now, add a sticky note with "LATER" on it.
- Place your information, draft or sticky note on the left-hand side of the middle row of the 'Build Team' view.

Assessment Matrix

The assessment matrix is a visualization of your value stream evaluations. It shows you the importance of your value streams (on the horizontal axis), as well as each stream's relative maturity or business readiness (on the vertical axis). In the example in Figure 41, the bubble size reflects the cost associated with each value stream.

The value stream assessment matrix uses the information from your analysis and visualizes the different pieces. It makes it easy to see how your different value streams compare to what you need to achieve your goals, and how they compare to each other.

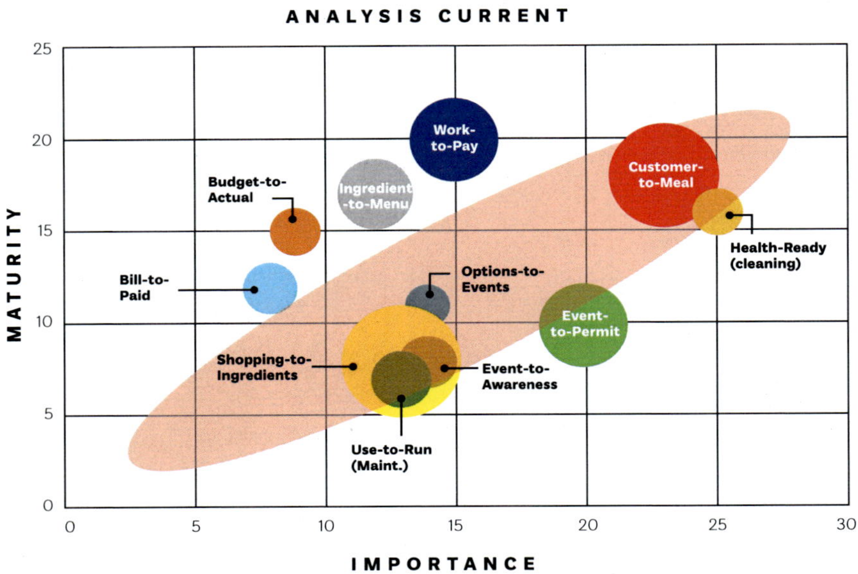

Figure 41 – Value stream assessment matrix for El Jefe

We will go into more detail of your assessment matrix in Part III of this book, but the *priority* of each value stream is determined by looking at your 'Create Customer' goals and metrics, and determining their dependence on the particular value stream. The *maturity* is determined by taking a critical, 'do-we-have-what-we-need' look at your people, processes, information, tools and technologies.

A rule of thumb is that the priority and maturity levels of your value streams should coincide. That means that the more important one of your value streams is, the more mature and the more business-ready it should be. This implies that there is a sweet spot that runs from the lower-left, to the upper-right corner of the matrix, as shown in Figure 41. As a general rule, your priority value streams should fall in this sweet spot.

If you have value streams that are very important, but less mature (i.e. in the lower right-hand quadrant), then it means they are not quite in the right state at the moment: they need to be matured. The 'Health-Ready (cleaning)' and 'Event-to-Permit' value streams are examples in Figure 41.

If your value streams are found in the upper-left quadrant, then it means they are more mature than you need them to be for your current set of customer-creation goals, metrics and initiatives. This may not be problematic, and we are not suggesting you make them less mature. However, if those value streams consume a lot of your resources – money, staff, etc., then you could consider reallocating some of those resources to other value streams that need to be strengthened.

In the Figure 41 example, we see that the 'Event-to-Permit' value stream is very important, but not that strong. On the other hand, the 'Work-to-Pay' value stream consumes a lot of resources (in terms of Carl's time). Carl could consider spending more time on the 'Event-to-Permit' stream, while offloading some of the 'Work-to-Pay' stream to his bookkeeper.[54]

TO DO

- If you have a document, worksheet or tool like the value stream assessment matrix already defined somewhere (in whatever form), collect, print or copy it. (Add the source information – whether it is an app, database, documentation, or even if it is in a person's head (including your own!).)
- If you don't, sketch it using the sample visualization – even on an envelope.
- Alternatively, you may choose to assign this task to someone who may be well-positioned to produce or draft your value stream assessment matrix – add it to a sticky note, and set up a meeting with the person to explain what you are looking for.

---

54 I was able to show a bookstore owner in the Upper Midwest of the United States that it was far better for her to hire someone to clean her bookstore so that she could spend more time on marketing activities. She had 'good-enough' data to show that her marketing activities had a clear impact on her sales.

- If you aren't in a position to do any of the above now, add a sticky note with "LATER" on it.
- Place your information, draft or sticky note in the middle section of the middle row of your 'Build Team' view.

Urgency

The urgency chart in the 'Build Team' view shows the relative urgency of fixing each value stream so that you can prioritize. It does this by combining the priority of the value stream with the size of the gap between its current and required maturity levels. The urgency chart is a good way to determine what you need to develop first, and where to spend your limited resources.

Figure 42 shows that the 'Event-to-Permit' value stream is the most urgent priority facing chef Carl's business.

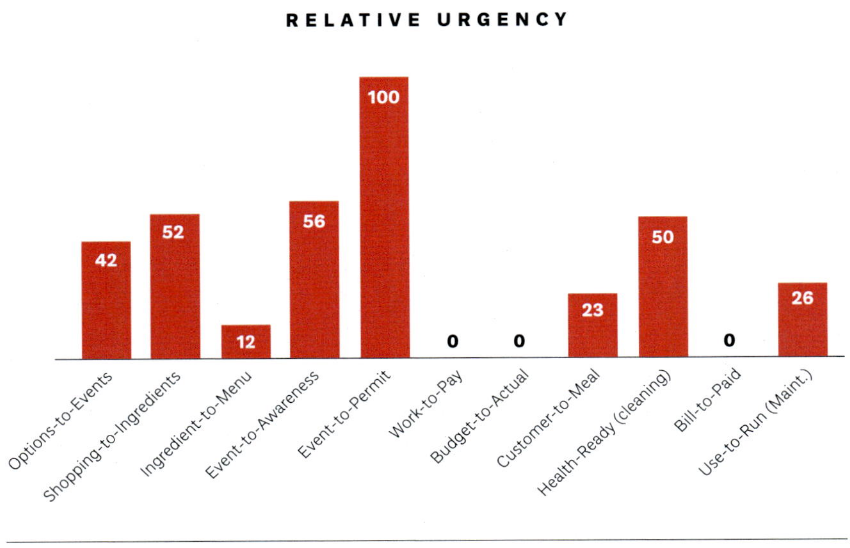

Figure 42 – Capability urgency for El Jefe

(In Chapter 16 we will show that a value stream's urgency is calculated by multiplying its importance by the size of the gap between its current and desired states. Again, it's not rocket science!)

TO DO

- If you have a document, worksheet or tool like the value stream urgency chart already defined somewhere (in whatever form), collect, print or copy it. (Add the source information – whether it is an app, database, documentation, or even if it is in a person's head (including your own!).)
- If you don't, sketch it using the sample visualization – even on an envelope.
- Alternatively, you may choose to assign this task to someone who may be well-positioned to produce or draft your value stream urgency chart – add it to a sticky note, and set up a meeting with the person to explain what you are looking for.
- If you aren't in a position to do any of the above now, add a sticky note with "LATER" on it.
- Place your information, draft or sticky note on the right-hand side of the middle row of your 'Build Team' view.

GOALS SECTION

The goals section of the 'Build Team' view helps you to define how you will close the gap between where your organization needs to be as a team, and where you find ourselves today.

It has three components:

1) goals and metrics,

2) roadmap, and

3) costs.

Let's look at each component in turn.

Goals and Metrics

Turning your goals and metrics[55] into reality depends on the quality of your initiatives and tasks.

Your goals and metrics will be monitored and managed for the duration of the goal cycle. This monitoring and management should enable you to adjust to any changing circumstances to achieve your goals.

The example for El Jefe in Figure 43 shows three specific goals needed to get the truck ready as a food truck: cleaning it so that it's ready for cooking, making sure it runs, and making sure that its kitchen functions properly. Each goal is represented by an orange bar. The gray bar shows the effort expended to reach the goal. The yellow bar shows the cost. For example, Carl planned to spend 10 hours on cleaning, but finished in 7 hours, so the gray 'Clean for Cooking' bar shows 70%. The yellow bar shows cost. It has come in at 113% for 'Clean for Cooking', so Carl spent more money on cleaning than he forecast.

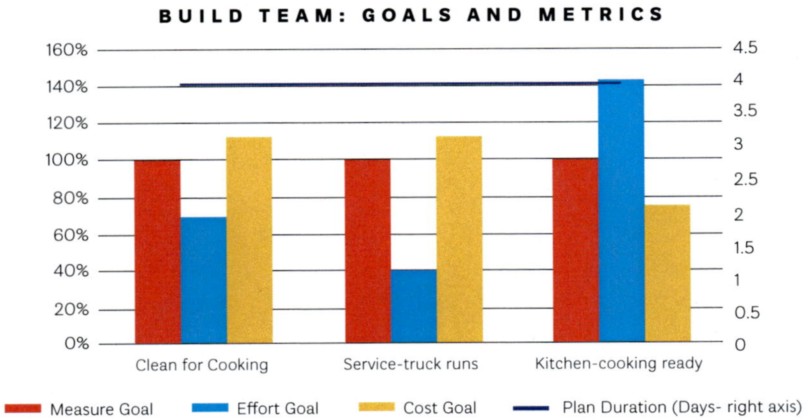

Figure 43 – Goals and metrics for El Jefe

55 I considered using the terms Objectives and Key Results, as described by John Doerr in *Measure What Matters* in 2018. These terms seem to have developed a life of their own, with all kinds of misunderstandings of them (and occasional resistance to them). The principle is exactly the same, and I find John's book a great reference for this topic.

TO DO

- If you have a document, worksheet or tool like the goals and metrics chart already defined somewhere (in whatever form), collect, print or copy it. (Add the source information – whether it is an app, database, documentation, or even if it is in a person's head (including your own!).)
- If you don't, sketch it using the sample visualization – even on an envelope.
- Alternatively, you may choose to assign this task to someone who may be well-positioned to produce or draft your organization's goals and metrics chart – add it to a sticky note, and set up a meeting with the person to explain what you are looking for.
- If you aren't in a position to do any of the above now, add a sticky note with "LATER" on it.
- Place your information, draft or sticky note on the left-hand side of the bottom row of your 'Build Team' view.

Roadmap

The 'Build Team' view contains a roadmap component, just like the 'Create Customer' view does. They are both visual calendar views. The purpose of both roadmaps is the same – to show you what is happening in each respective view, and when it's happening. They are good tools to:

- get everyone in your organization on the same page,
- consider how the different parts of your organization need to be coordinated,
- consider how the different tasks of your organization need to be sequenced,
- track progress (and the speed of your progress), and
- manage your resources, etc.

(I am assuming that you are using a task management, project management or agile tool to plan your efforts, including the resources that you will need. Most of these come with a roadmap view or a Gantt chart.)

It's highly likely that you will have some projects that are intended to improve your organization. If you do, they go in your 'Build Teams' roadmap. You may have 'Build Team' initiatives that are built into your 'Create Customer' initiatives. There is no need to artificially move them to this area, unless there is an obvious benefit.

Goals	Items	Date		Plan Duration	1.6	2.6	3.6	4.6	5.6	6.6	7.6	8.6	9.6	10.6
		Start	Target											
TRUCK READY		01.06.14	04.06.14											
	Clean for Cooking	01.06.14	04.06.14	4										
	Service - truck runs	01.06.14	04.06.14	4										
	Kitchen - cooking ready	01.06.14	04.06.14	4										

Figure 44 – 'Build Team' roadmap for El Jefe

TO DO

- If you have a document, worksheet or tool like the 'Build Team' roadmap already defined somewhere (in whatever form), collect, print or copy it. (Add the source information – whether it is an app, database, documentation, or even if it is in a person's head (including your own!).)
- If you don't, sketch it using the sample visualization – even on an envelope.
- Alternatively, you may choose to assign this task to someone who may be well-positioned to produce or draft your roadmap – add it to a sticky note, and set up a meeting with the person to explain what you are looking for.
- If you aren't in a position to do any of the above now, add a sticky note with "LATER" on it.

- Place your information, draft or sticky note in the middle of the bottom row of your 'Build Team' view.

Costs

Your initiatives (and tasks) will form a cornerstone of your cost chart. It will show you how much each of your goals, metrics and/or initiatives will cost.

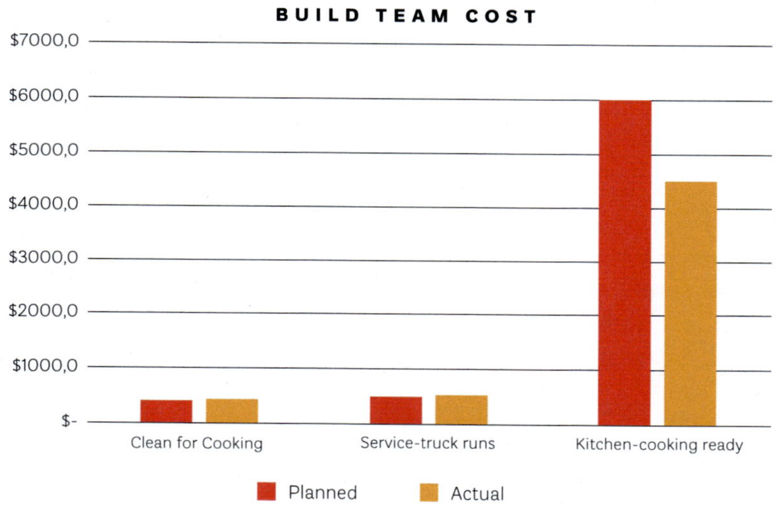

Figure 45 – 'Build Team' costs for El Jefe

TO DO

- If you have a document, worksheet or tool containing your cost chart somewhere (in whatever form), collect, print or copy it. (Add the source information – whether it is an app, database, documentation, or even if it is in a person's head (including your own!).)
- If you don't, sketch it using the sample visualization – even on an envelope.

- Alternatively, you may choose to assign this task to someone who may be well-positioned to produce or draft your cost chart – add it to a sticky note, and set up a meeting with the person to explain what you are looking for.
- If you aren't in a position to do any of the above now, add a sticky note with "LATER" on it.
- Place your information, draft or sticky note on the right-hand side of the bottom row of your 'Build Team' view.

> **Your best strategies – even your most wonderful market segment/s where you have a clear shot at an uncontested field – will simply remain ideas if you don't build a team who can implement them effectively.**
>
> **It is therefore critical to build and develop the right team with the right capabilities to deliver the right value streams to your customers. With the right team, the right capabilities (people, processes, information, tools and technologies) and the right value streams, you are setting your organization up for success.**
>
> **The 'Build Team' elements of your visible mission will give you the tools to figure out what you have now, and what you need to develop to achieve your goals.**
>
> **As you continue to develop your team every year, you can build an amazing organization that will impress and excite your customers, again and again.**
>
> **And as an added bonus, you will frustrate (and be the envy of) your competition!**

NASA built an organization that enabled it to achieve success with each of its space missions. Its organization has evolved as its space program has evolved, including participating in the International Space Station, planetary probes, solar probes, and even missions where probes have exited our solar system.

Similar to NASA, you need to make sure that you have the right team to achieve what you envision. If you are going to record "Kind of Blue", you need Miles Davis and John Coltrane. For Beethoven's Fifth Symphony, you need a full-blown symphony orchestra, and for the Ninth you'd better get your hands on a choir as well!

So far in the book, we have looked at:

- your vision,
- your organization,
- your competitive landscape,
- understanding which markets you are going to engage with, and
- the organization you need to build or develop.

The last two views that we have covered in your visible mission ('Create Customer' and 'Build Team') have both involved goals, metrics and initiatives to achieve your goals. These two sets of goals, metrics and initiatives will be combined and used to monitor your progress towards your collective mission.

It's important to know and expect that reality will inevitably be different from what your plans assume. In order to adjust to unfolding realities, you need to continually monitor your progress and decide what your next and best options are. In the next chapter, you will see how you can monitor your progress by using the 'Mission and Progress' view of your visible mission.

'BUILD TEAM' WORKSHEET

Business Capabilities	Value Streams
Who: Where: Target Date:	Who: Where: Target Date:

Analysis	Matrix	Urgency
Who: Where: Target Date:	Who: Where: Target Date:	Who: Where: Target Date:

Goal and Metrics	Roadmap	Cost
Who: Where: Target Date:	Who: Where: Target Date:	Who: Where: Target Date:

Note that a digital version of this worksheet can be downloaded from the book's website (www.thevisiblemission.com).

CHAPTER 9

Vision and Progress View: Progress

Chapter 4 outlined the 'Vision' component of the 'Vision and Progress' view of your visible mission. Now that we have explained the other three views, it's time to outline the 'Progress' component of your 'Vision and Progress' view.

NASA selected its Moon landing mission, established its goals and planned its execution. It also planned the development of its organizational capabilities necessary to achieve its goals. Their plans were based on earlier work and future assumptions. NASA then executed their mission. As part of the execution, they measured their progress and monitored the conditions they faced. That's because plans and assumptions (no matter how detailed they may be) are never a substitute for reality during a strategy's execution.

Mike Tyson once said: "Everybody has a plan until they get punched in the mouth".[56] That doesn't mean that we don't need to plan. On the contrary, it means that we're likely to get punched in the mouth, and we have to know what to do when it happens!

As a plan's execution unfolds, there are usually a lot of 'things' happening, and a lot of information that needs to be managed. Those relevant 'things' and information need to be evaluated, decided upon, and in some cases, acted upon.

---

56 Before his fight with Evander Holyfield, February 1990.

The Mission Control Center was where NASA's primary monitoring was taking place. It was where information was collected and placed in the right context, which then helped with decision-making and plan adjustments.

Similarly, when you have all of your information collected in one combined view in your own mission control center (i.e. your visible mission), it's possible for you to start recognizing what information is critical to your organization (that you might have missed before), as well as what information may be largely irrelevant (which you may have thought was urgent or critical before you developed your visible mission).

The 'Progress' component of your 'Vision and 'Progress' view will show your planned route (your roadmap), your current state, and your trajectory.

> **A goal with a plan to achieve it where progress isn't monitored is useless. It's a daydream.**
>
> **Reality will always be different to all of your plan's assumptions. In order to succeed, you need to understand how you are progressing, and any changing conditions. You need to be able to identify if changes are having an impact on your plans. This monitoring information will enable you to react appropriately to achieve your goals.**

You are here.

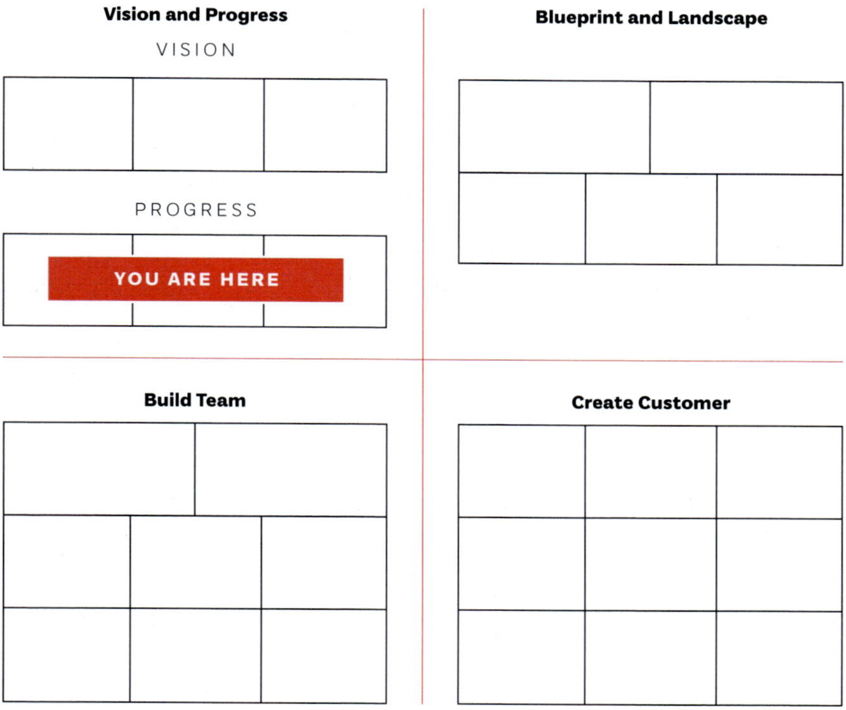

Figure 46 – You are here. There is a 'Progress' worksheet at the end of the chapter (and online at www.thevisiblemission.com) for you to use to develop your own visible mission.

As I shared with you in Chapter 4, imagine walking into your own mission control room. You have four walls (or four views on one wall), and each of the views contains the visualized information you and your team needs to observe, contextualize, decide and act (both individually as well as collectively).

The primary view of your visible mission (mission control room) is your 'Vision and Progress' view. The progress section is the bottom row of the 'Vision and Progress' view. This is where you track your efforts to make sure that your moonshot happens, and where you can react appropriately by observing any changing realities. Your visible mission provides you with a framework to help you contextualize your information. It enables you to have access to the information needed to make high-quality decisions, and to act quickly (but deliberately and thoughtfully).

PROGRESS SECTION

The 'Create Customer' and 'Build Team' views are where you create goals, metrics, and initiatives to achieve your goals. The progress section of the 'Vision and Progress' view is where the progress you are making towards achieving your goals is shown. It has three components:

1) roadmap,

2) current status, and

3) progress.

Let's look at each of these components in turn.

Combined Roadmap

All of the goals and initiatives that you have defined in your 'Create Customer' and 'Build Team' views are also shown here. The roadmap is the equivalent of the route that you plan to take to achieve your goals. It is a visual calendar view, and it's a good tool to get everyone in your organization on the same page, to consider how the different parts and tasks in your organization need to be coordinated and sequenced, to track your progress (and the speed of your progress), and to manage your resources, etc. It shows where you stand within your planned initiatives.

Your roadmap helps to keep you on track by making sure that you reach intermediate points along the way to achieving your goals as and when you need to. Reaching intermediate points is often required to prepare for subsequent phases or initiatives. For example, if you want to make sure that your customer support service is working well before you deploy your new app.

Having a route helps to keep us focused and disciplined. In my experience, organizational plans can be easily derailed by developments like a new business opportunity, a new technology, or an innovative approach to solve a customer problem. Having a roadmap allows us to look at developments like these and consider whether we should stick with our current plan, or adjust it to accommodate the new development. We may decide to include the emerging issue in our next goal cycle, so we can address it then rather than now. Or we may decide that it falls outside what we are delivering to our customers, and therefore we won't act on it at all.

Goals	Items	Date		Plan Duration	1.6	2.6	3.6	4.6	5.6	6.6
		Start	Target							
TRUCK READY		00.01.00	00.01.00							
	Clean for Cooking	01.06.14	04.06.14	4						
	Service - truck runs	01.06.14	04.06.14	4						
	Kitchen - cooking ready	01.06.14	04.06.14	4						
TEST COOKING		06.06.14	11.06.14							
	Buy Food	06.06.14	11.06.14	6						
	Develop Menu	06.06.14	11.06.14	6						
	Cook - Lummus Beach	06.06.14	11.06.14	6						
NEW ORLEANS		13.06.14	18.06.14							
	Buy Food	13.06.14	18.06.14	7						
	Develop Menu	13.06.14	18.06.14	7						
	Cook - Cafe du Monde	13.06.14	18.06.14	7						

Figure 47 – A combined roadmap for El Jefe

TO DO

- If you have a document, worksheet or tool like the combined roadmap above already defined somewhere (in whatever form), collect, print or copy it. (Add the source information – whether it is an app, database, documentation, or even if it is in a person's head (including your own!).)
- If you don't, sketch it using the sample visualization – even on an envelope.
- Alternatively, you may choose to assign this task to someone who may be well-positioned to produce or draft your combined roadmap – add it to a sticky note, and set up a meeting with the person, to explain what you are looking for.
- If you aren't in a position to do any of the above now, add a sticky note with "LATER" on it.
- Place your information, draft or sticky note on the left-hand side of the 'Progress' row of the 'Vision and Progress' view.

Current Status

To achieve your goals, you need to make sure that you assign and use your resources responsibly. The status section of the 'Progress' section of the 'Vision and Progress' shows you three things:

1) your current progress towards your goal,

2) the amount of time you have left to achieve your goal,

3) the amount of money planned and used so far.

The status section is intended to help you to coordinate your time and money to reach your goals.

A large deviation between any of these three aspects will allow your team to identify and discuss the reasons, and whether adjustments are needed to address the situation. In some cases, deviations will be normal – for example, some efforts will need upfront expenses, while others will lag with their expenses. The primary idea is to make the three aspects visible, and to prompt discussion when needed.

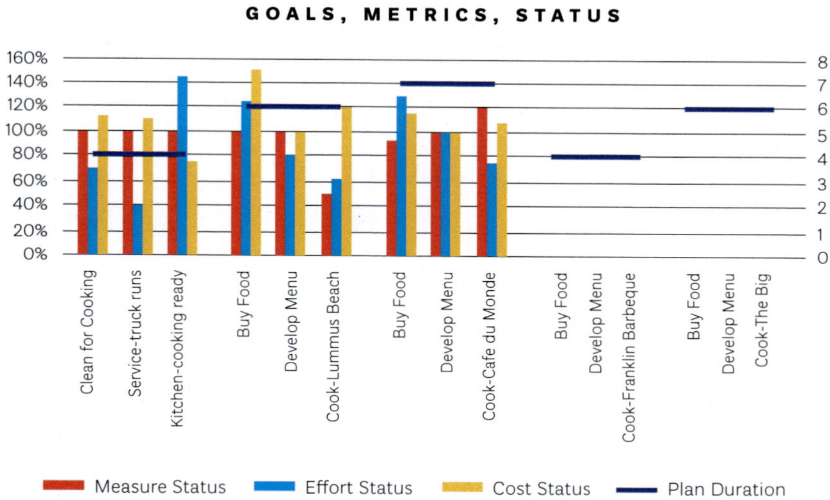

Figure 48 – Current status for El Jefe

TO DO

- If you have a document, worksheet, or tool containing status information like the above somewhere (in whatever form), collect, print or copy it. (Add the source information – whether it is an app, database, documentation, or even if it is in a person's head (including your own!).)
- If you don't, sketch it using the sample visualization – even on an envelope.
- Alternatively, you may choose to assign this task to someone who may be well-positioned to produce or draft your current status – add it to a sticky note, and set up a meeting with the person to explain what you are looking for.
- If you aren't in a position to do any of the above now, add a sticky note with "LATER" on it.
- Place your information, draft or sticky note in the middle of the 'Progress' row of the 'Vision and Progress' view.

Progress

The 'Progress' section is rounded out by the progress screen itself. As the name indicates, this screen shows you how your efforts have progressed over time. It uses the goal metric, calendar and cost variables as its measures. You can think of this screen as the status over time.

Showing your current state in the context of your earlier progress may help you see if your progress is stalling, or even if you are actually moving away from your goal. It makes the situation visible, and enables you to decide whether or not to add more resources to help you achieve your goal.

The example shown in Figure 49 indicates that the first four goals were achieved by El Jefe in very short order, over three weeks each. However, achieving the goal for Los Angeles took longer. Graphing your goal achievement trends is useful to help you see how you are performing over time, so you can plan better to improve the way you and your team work, etc.

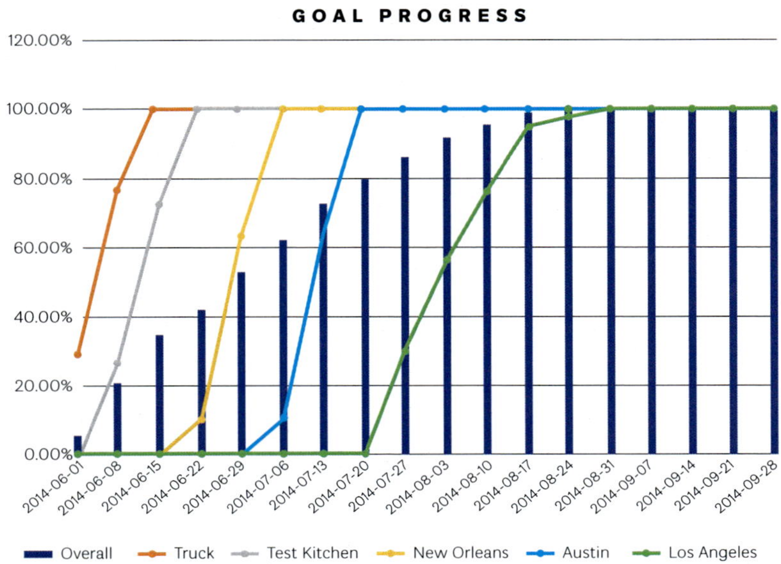

Figure 49 – Progress for El Jefe

TO DO

- If you have a document, worksheet or tool that has your progress information somewhere (in whatever form), collect, print or copy it. (Add the source information – whether it is an app, database, documentation, or even if it is in a person's head (including your own!).)
- If you don't, sketch it using the sample visualization – even on an envelope.
- Alternatively, you may choose to assign this task to someone who may be well-positioned to produce or draft your progress information – add it to a sticky note, and set up a meeting with the person to explain what you are looking for.
- If you aren't in a position to do any of the above, add a sticky note with "LATER" on it.
- Place your information, draft or sticky note on the right-hand side of the 'Progress' row of the 'Vision and Progress' view.

A plan on our way to a goal means nothing without knowing if we are moving forward.

Having a roadmap, knowing your current status, and an indication of the progress you have made over time shows you how you are doing. When you are not moving along as you planned, you will have all the information you need to determine the best response to your situation. It will allow you to actively navigate towards your goal.

You have to expect that things are not going to go exactly according to your plan. However, having an awareness of your situation will help you to react appropriately, and make timely adjustments when necessary.

NASA used its Mission Control Center to track, understand, decide and act (or instruct what needed to be done) as its missions unfolded. It had to constantly adapt to unfolding realities. For example, when the oxygen tank failed during the Apollo 13 mission, the mission was aborted. NASA adjusted. The Apollo 13 astronauts looped around the Moon (instead of landing there as originally intended), and NASA's Mission Control Center helped to guide them safely back to Earth.

We have now looked at all four views of your visible mission (your mission control center).

The parts of your organization are closely interrelated and interdependent. This isn't business theory, it's business practice – your vision informs your business model, your environment exists and evolves, your ability to create customers determines your survival, and you need a team to make things happen (i.e. achieve your goals). You need to determine what to do, and then to monitor and adjust as necessary.

In the next chapter (The Whole and the Parts), we will take a closer look at how the parts of your organization are interrelated, and what that means to you in terms of running your organization.

'PROGRESS' WORKSHEET

Roadmap	Status	Progress
Who: Where: Target Date:	Who: Where: Target Date:	Who: Where: Target Date:

Note that a digital version of this worksheet can be downloaded from the book's website (www.thevisiblemission.com).

CHAPTER 10

The Whole and The Parts

NASA's Mission Control Center managed almost unimaginable complexity by identifying, collecting, and unifying the critical aspects of their missions. It didn't just passively observe the unfolding of its plans and changing realities. It wasn't involved in a spectator sport.

Instead, NASA's Mission Control Center was a critical participant. Its staff observed and oriented their perspective to enable them to see everything that was necessary to make high-quality decisions, and then they acted (or issued instructions to act).

The success of the Apollo space program was achieved by the contribution of hundreds[57] of thousands of people who were ultimately coordinated by NASA's Mission Control Center.

As you develop your own mission control center via your visible mission, you will be able to similarly coordinate your vision, goals and organization.

We have been looking at the structure and the different parts of your visible mission. By now you have also seen that you already have many of the parts that are necessary to successfully manage strategy.

Let me tell you a story about parts and how they make up the whole.

Ever since I was little, I have loved cycling. I remember having a chain-driven tricycle that I used for all kinds of stunts. Inevitably I had some accidents, although they were more related to non-stunts than

57 At its height, the Apollo space program employed 400,000 people, with 20,000 organizations supporting its activities. https:/en.wikipedia.org/wiki/Apollo_program

the other way around. I had to wait until I was in 10th grade for a bicycle because my father thought the steep roads in the town where I grew up were too dangerous. When I finally got one, I loved the sense of speed, the wind on my skin, the power I felt in my legs, the sweat, and the sense of being alive!

What makes cycling so much fun is not the equipment as such. Neither is it the fact that there are wheels involved, or that there's a steering mechanism.

A bicycle standing in the shed is not that much fun either. Neither are the individual parts.

Cycling is fun when the wheels, the steering, the chain and your own body all merge into a single activity – when you get on the bicycle and start riding. When you are getting fitter, stronger, faster, and feel that you can go forever!

Figure 50 – Bicycle parts

Figure 51 – Cycling

Running a business is clearly complex. Lots of moving parts are connected and interdependent, whether we acknowledge that fact or not. This sense of complexity dissuades many CEOs from managing strategy in a consistent, coherent manner.

The visible mission structure enables you to manage the critical sets of information needed to observe and orient your organization. However, your organization is more than the sum of its parts. Its parts need to move together in a clear and coordinated way. Your visible mission will enable you to make high-quality and timely decisions, giving you the ability to act quickly (but deliberately).

As we walked through the different views, sections and elements of your visible mission in the earlier chapters, you likely identified the connections between your different parts.

If you ignore these interdependencies, it's easy to make a decision about one aspect without fully appreciating the implications it may have on other aspects of your organization. For example, your 'Create Customer' plan might depend heavily on a particular function you're your customer relationship management system. If the tool for that CRM function is old, fragmented and slow, then you may be setting your organization up for failure, unless you address the issue appropriately.

There is no prescriptive approach to managing interdependencies, but having all of the relevant information in front of you makes it easier to keep your organization's connections and interdependencies in your working memory. This ease of access, coupled with the visibility of your interdependencies will enable you and your team to become what we can appropriately call 'strategically fluent'.

Being strategically fluent means that you not only able to analyze the strategic aspects of your organization and to plan and execute, but that you also have a map to place relevant information, regardless of whether that information is internal to your organization, or if it relates to your competition, your customers, or any other external influence. Mapping relevant information enables you to determine its implications (or potential implications) for your organization a lot faster.

The visible mission allows you to continuously use and update your map by:

- placing and connecting information,
- communicating more clearly,
- determining what your options are, and
- ultimately deciding whether or not to act, or to wait.

Figure 52 shows a basic visual representation of potential organizational interdependencies.

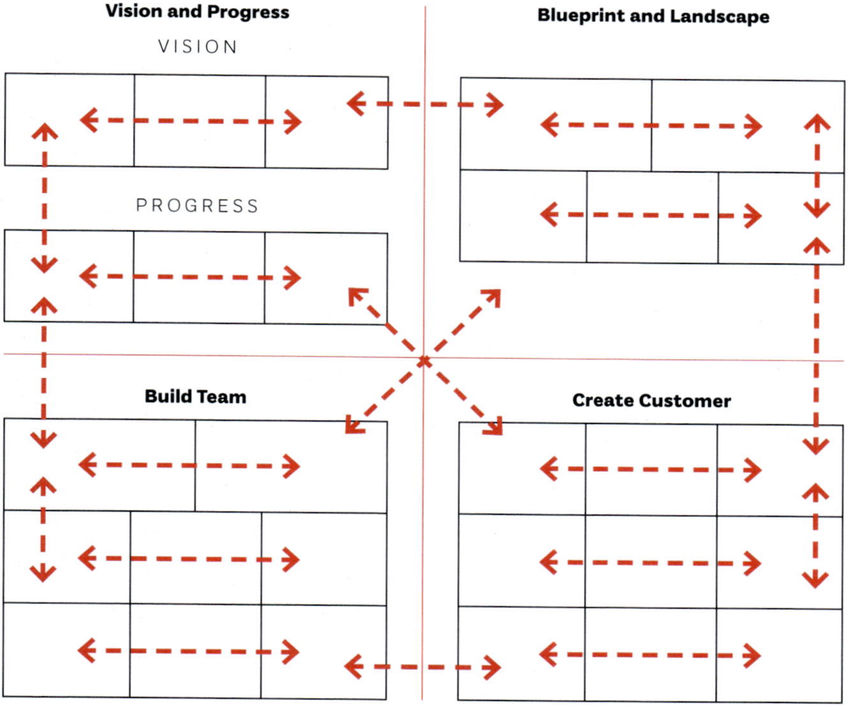

Figure 52 – Some potential organizational interdependencies

Your *vision and mission* provide the context for your *business model*, although your business model should support your mission. Your business model should enable your collective '*Create Customer*' and '*Build Team*' aspects. Both of these should reflect the information that is contextualized by your *competitive landscape*, as well as your *future landscape*.

Your '*Create Customer*' aspect is both dependent on your *team* (and your '*Build Team*' aspect), while your '*Build Team*' aspect is infused by what is planned in your '*Create Customer*' aspect.

The '*Create Customer*' and '*Build Team*' *aspects* share a largely similar structure: definition, analysis and plan. Your definition sets the context for your analysis, and your analysis provides your options and information to help you decide on your goals, metrics and plans. Your goals, metrics and plans in both areas are coordinated internally and with each other.

The *progress* towards achieving your goals, your metrics and your initiatives in both aspects drive coherently forward to not only help you succeed with your goal cycle, but to progress towards your *vision*.

Knowing what the different views of your visible mission describe and contain, as well as how they work together, ultimately enables you to contextualize information faster. This ability to observe unfolding realities as well as your internal visibility also enables you to react more sure-footedly and faster. (For example, the visible mission could enable you to consider artificial intelligence in terms of its contribution to your customer insights, as part of your products, or as a capability and/or resource that you could develop or consider in greater detail during your next goal cycle.)

If you combine this information with an inspiring vision and a team that is informed and aligned, then you will develop into a formidable competitor, regardless of your field.

Having your elements visible is not enough. You also need to make their relationships and interdependencies clear and obvious.

Your visible mission will enable you to develop strategic fluency by keeping your key elements visible. This will allow you, your team and your partners to observe, contextualize, decide and act on the latest relevant information.

The visible mission is not a spectator sport. It enables you to actively participate and steer toward success.

NASA didn't say that their missions were too complicated to manage, coordinate, execute, monitor and adjust. They also didn't say that they were going to plan some of their missions, but then 'wing' certain aspects of them. They didn't put their heads in the sand and just hope that things would work out with hard work and dedication.

Instead, their Mission Control Center played a crucial role in managing the complexity their missions faced, and dealing with a hostile and often unpredictable environment.

Since you are running a business (even if you are just starting out), you already have some of your 'parts' in place. Maybe some of the 'connecting tissue' may be missing, but we will get to that later in the book.

After you have created and populated your own mission control center (your visible mission), you will use it to run your organization. You will consistently experience how exciting it is to:

- work towards your goals.
- convert the power of ideas into activity and effort.
- steer across challenging terrain and unpredictable environments, and
- use your brakes effectively where and when needed.

This chapter concludes the structural description of your visible mission. We have seen that it consists of four views:

1) your 'Vision and Progress' view,

2) your 'Blueprint and Landscape' view,

3) your 'Create Customer' view, and

4) your 'Build Team' view.

In this chapter, we saw how all the parts (views) fit together to form the whole. You have collected the parts you have, and drafted out parts where appropriate. Perhaps you have also planned to develop your missing parts. You may have enough of your visible mission in place to take it for a 'drive'. In the next chapter, we will see how you can do that!

CHAPTER 11

Steering Towards Success

NASA didn't use their Mission Control Center for the first time during the Moon landing mission: it was a part of all of their space missions. It was one of the capabilities that was developed and improved as the Apollo space program progressed.

You have already put together some (or maybe even most) of the parts of your mission control center (your visible mission). While that is a necessary start, it's not enough.

A bicycle only realizes its full potential when its parts are connected and can be used for cycling. In the same way, your visible mission's reason for existence is to connect your organizational parts properly, and to use them to guide you toward successful goal cycles.

You have by now a (partially) functional visible mission. Looking at it means little. You need to use it to steer towards success. Some think strategy management is about developing static plans that are presented, shelved and then forgotten.

Instead, you need to press the proverbial 'START' button with your visible mission!

You have at least some of your visible mission elements in place – now we are going to start having fun!

Steering your organization is like driving: it's a combination of observing and acting. Yes, it takes some practice, and some getting used to. There is also a need to truly understand what you are seeing, and to be able to place it in the right context.

For example, you may see deer along the road, and you know to slow down. There is no way of telling whether it will run away or cross the road. So you slow down until you are past it. This is an example of observing a situation, contextualizing what you see, deciding, and then acting.

With driving, we pick a destination, and along the way we observe and adjust as necessary. After a few years of driving, we do this automatically. Our experience and ability allow us to deal with new situations more comfortably, and with a better likelihood of a good outcome. For example, driving in a storm at night is far more manageable for an experienced driver than for someone who is learning to drive.

Steering and guiding your organization is far more complicated than driving. Your visible mission will act like a cockpit that you can use to observe your organization and your environment. It will also enable you to steer your organization more easily towards achieving your defined goals.

WHAT YOU HAVE

I hope you have made use of the opportunity to capture and/or collect the elements of your visible mission that you already have. I also hope you have drafted out some of the elements that you are missing.

I want you to look at the visible mission you have started to assemble. You may be thinking that it's too early and that you don't have everything in place.

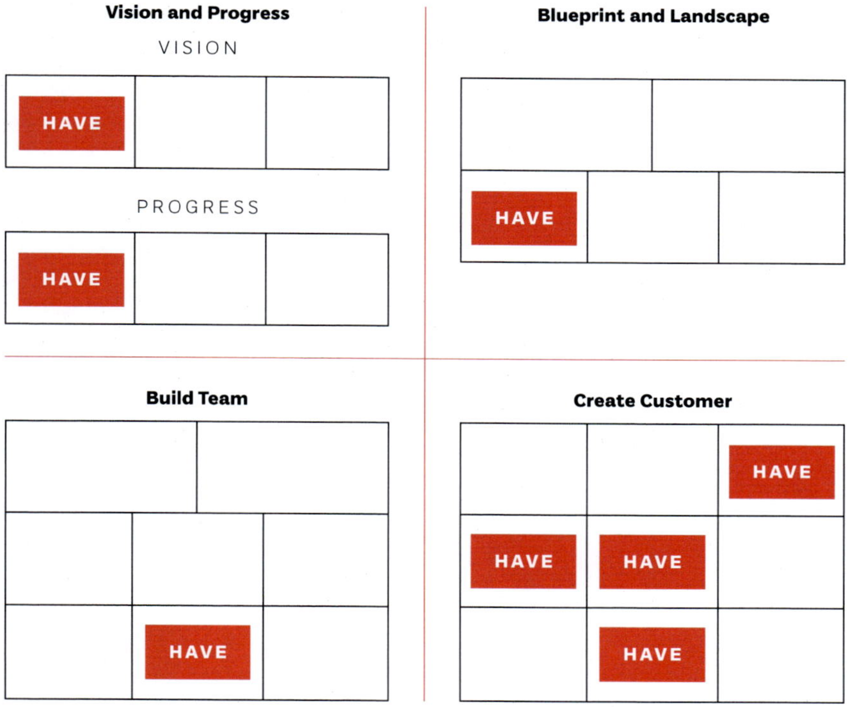

Figure 53 – 'What you have' example for a visible mission

The visible mission 'what you have' example shown in Figure 53 may not be that far off from what you currently have. You are likely to have a vision on your website, and a set of projects. You are also likely to have your products/services documented, as well as your customer segments and locations. You might have projects related to your customers, and maybe a project that is intended to replace an internal system, as well as some employee development plans, etc.

This is also a good time to consider the visible mission sections that you marked for "Later". Taking a step back, which of these would you like to get in place before going further? Who do you want to take part in discussing each one? Instead of overthinking them, get a meeting scheduled, and get a draft in place for each one.

Maybe all of your parts aren't well integrated yet, but it's a start. You already have a lot to work with!

WHERE YOU ARE HEADING

I want you to imagine the following scenario for a moment.

You are walking your team through your visible mission and explaining each view aspect of your organization, your rationale for your business model, and the visibility that each of your views provides. You are walking your team through the choices both you and they have made in relation to your customer segments, products and markets.

Imagine talking to your team about:

- value streams,
- capabilities, and
- opportunities to improve.

Imagine meeting with your team on a regular basis to:

- track your progress,
- take a clear look at your internal and external environments, and
- decide on necessary adjustments.

Imagine meeting with your team, seeing how you are progressing, and ultimately achieving the goals that you have set.

What you have just imagined is right there within your grasp!

You have the opportunity to start using your visible mission to define, develop, plan, execute, track and adjust your missions, so that you can bring your vision to life.

With your visible mission, you are now in a custom-made cockpit for your organization. But in practical terms, how do you use it?

You can start by introducing your visible mission to your team – explaining what it is, and what they should expect from it.

INTRODUCING THE VISIBLE MISSION TO YOUR TEAM

You should introduce your visible mission to your team before your first monitoring meeting. You may also choose to share it with a small group, perhaps with your leadership team first. This will give them a preview, and they can help with the wider organizational communication of it. Of course, if there are pieces of information that you would not want to share with everyone in your organization, you get to decide what you leave out.

Explaining the Visible Mission's Purpose

It's important to explain that the purpose of using your visible mission is to help your organization to define success, and to track and steer you all towards success. Share the visible mission information that you have already collected. If your visible mission is not completely populated, explain that you will be building it out as a team. You may ask for team members to volunteer to contribute.

Explain that the different views will be used to:

- collect and share information,
- analyze your internal and external realities,
- plan and coordinate work,
- monitor and steer your organization toward success.

MONITOR AND STEERING

Once you have introduced the visible mission to your team, monitoring and steering are the key ongoing tasks. There are a number of issues to decide before your monitoring and steering meetings are planned and scheduled.

Determining Meeting Frequency

Depending on your type of business, industry, operating experience, and the general circumstances you face, you may have weekly, fortnightly or monthly monitoring and steering meetings. I do not suggest holding them less frequently than monthly. If you do, you will lose the sense of working as a team towards a common purpose.

In fact, weekly might be a good place to start. If you keep your meetings tight, you can learn how to conduct them quickly and effectively with a little practice. Once you are up and running and on top of things, you can make your monitoring and steering meetings fortnightly or monthly. If anything happens that has a significant impact on your organization or your plans, then you could have more frequent meetings. For example, during COVID-19, more frequent meetings may be necessary as your circumstances change.

Who Should Lead and Who Should Attend?

Ultimately, this is your organizational cockpit. You are the pilot. You set the tone, the expectations and the example. You introduce your visible mission agenda, and hand it over to the people who are responsible for each of your initiatives. Attendance requirements need to be practical, but if possible, invite your entire team.

Scheduling Your Meetings

It's important to recognize that your ongoing visible mission meetings have two components:

1) monitoring, and
2) steering.

The meetings are not just about monitoring your progress. They also provide you with the opportunity to steer by deciding:

- what you need to keep on doing,
- what you need to change, and
- what you need to stop doing.

These meetings also have a social aspect where you acknowledge your team's commitment and effort in achieving the goals you set on the way to realizing your mission.

Every time you receive important new information (e.g. a new trend, or a change in your competition), record it in the appropriate view of your visible mission. Doing this continues to make the invisible visible, and it helps your team become familiar with how to understand, think and react to the external environment, even if you are not in the room.

Meeting Agenda

Here is the agenda I recommend for a visible mission monitoring and steering meeting.

- Welcome your team and set the context for your meeting.
- Raise urgent strategic developments that affect your mission, goals and initiatives.
- Team progress reports.
- Make decisions – what needs to start, change or stop.
- Assign actions – who does what, and by when.
- Non-urgent 'Blueprint and Landscape' updates.
- Next meeting reminder.

Let's look at each of these agenda items in turn.

Welcome

Welcome your team to your meeting. Remind them that they are important players in making the work happen to achieve your collective goals. This is a team effort, and you all have a common purpose. Use your 'Vision and Progress' view to focus your team's attention. Be authentic and honest with your team.

Raise Urgent Strategic Developments

Provide your own assessment of actual, active threats and opportunities in relation to your choices of goals, metrics and initiatives.

This should be done before any progress reporting takes place in the meeting, because it provides the context within which the reporting needs to take place. This is especially important if there is the possibility or the realization that some initiatives, metrics or even goals may have to be canceled or redirected.

For example, during COVID-19, restaurants, hotels and most retailers had to reconsider what they were doing. If a restaurant had plans to re-do its menu, or had a summer or Christmas initiative, those plans would likely have had to be scrapped or potentially redone.

Opportunities might have emerged during COVID-19 as well. If you are an e-commerce business, it may have created opportunities for your organization. If your original plans were focused elsewhere, or you were only expecting organic growth, then your plans may have needed to scrapped or adapted.

As you talk about strategic developments like these, visualize them for your team by placing them in the emerging future and industry assessment sections in your 'Blueprint and Landscape' view. When developments are affecting your customers, your channels, and/or your suppliers, point those things out to your team as well.

Team Progress Reports

These provide an internal view of how your organization is performing.

Each of your team leaders that are responsible for a particular goal, metric and initiative should share their progress, any problems they face, and what they need to succeed. If there are large differences between the relevant visual mission calendar, cost and goal metrics, then make sure you understand the reasons why by asking your team leaders to explain. For example, if team progress is stalling, probe to understand why that is the case.

Obviously, this should be explained by referring to the current state of your 'Progress' section, by talking about your roadmap, current status and progress.

Make Decisions

Following the progress reporting, identify decisions that need to be made in terms of what you need to start doing, what you need to adjust, and what you need to stop doing. If it's not possible to make these decisions in the meeting itself, note that they need to be made. Assign the decision-making responsibility to the most appropriate person or people.

Assign Actions

Assign the actions that are needed to implement your meeting decisions to a specific person or team, and set a target date. In other words, outline:

- what needs to be done,
- who needs to do it, and
- when it needs to be done by.

Non-Urgent Blueprint and Landscape Updates

Discuss any non-urgent observations since your last meeting in relation to your industry, your competition, and any developing trends. Encourage your team members to keep their eyes and ears open for any of these things.

However, when something is noticed, it's important to analyze and discuss potential implications. For example, it's not sufficient to report that "artificial intelligence is growing" without also reporting any potential implications for your organization, such as "and it is plausible that it may affect our ability to do XYZ".

If there is a decision to act on any 'Blueprint and Landscape' updates, even if it's just "keep your eyes on this" or "get it on the next goal cycle", make sure that the task is assigned to a person or team.

Next Meeting Reminder

Thank everyone for their attendance at your visible mission meeting, and remind your team when your next meeting is. As I mentioned earlier, it takes some practice to make your meetings effective. You will see the worth of them when you do.

Now that we are at this point in the book, I would like you to take a look at what you have been able to put together so far. I hope you are pleased with what you already have, excited about filling the possible gaps, and excited about putting your visible mission into practice.

> **Your visible mission only has purpose if it is used to steer your organization towards achieving your goals. If the goal planning is defining your moonshot, then your monitoring meeting is tracking and steering your mission to and from your metaphorical moon.**

NASA did not start using their Mission Control Center for their first Moon landing mission. They built, tested, and then implemented their Mission Control Center before the first mission in the Apollo space program, knowing that it would be valuable, even that it would improve over time.

You are now ready to power up your own mission control center (your visible mission) to help you to steer your organization towards success. This will not just be a test flight, it will become an ongoing part of helping you to achieve your goals. You can use your visible mission to guide and inspire your team, keep them focused, help them adjust when needed, and help them to work together very clearly and effectively.

Part II of this book has largely been about the visible mission structure, its parts, and how they all fit together. In this chapter, you got the first taste of how to actively use it.

In Part III, we will go into more detail about the process of developing, analyzing, planning and executing your visible mission. We will be looking at world-class tools that most leading organizations are using. We will start by looking at the vision roadmap.

PART THREE

The Making of Your Moonshot

CHAPTER 12

How Planning Works

US President Kennedy set out the vision for NASA's Apollo space program – to take people to the Moon and back. This vision was achieved via a series of missions that progressed from launching unmanned space flights through to putting astronauts into space, then into orbit, and finally landing on the Moon and returning safely. Each mission was defined, analyzed, planned, and particular goals were set. NASA was prepared, and its Mission Control Center was used to progressively move the organization closer to achieving its vision.

In Part II you have established the structure of your own mission control center. You have added the elements you have, and drafted the elements that you need. Maybe you have already started using your mission control center.

If you have, this is a great beginning!

Your mission control center really comes to life when you have an inspiring vision and when you use high-quality tools along the way towards achieving it. As you have seen in Part II, you are using some of these tools already.

Part III will show you how to use the different visible mission views to create, plan, execute, build, track and adjust your missions and goals using the best tools available today. [58]

---

58 I expect some of these tools to be replaced by better tools and techniques in the future, and when that happens, I hope you will replace the older ones as you continue to use your own mission control center.

> **Having a vision is a wonderful opportunity to provide inspiration to your team.**
>
> **You realize your vision via a series of goal cycles. For each goal cycle, you analyze your situation, set achievable goals and metrics, define and execute initiatives, and steer your organization towards success.**
>
> **You do this over and over, every time moving towards your vision.**

I introduced the reasons why you need a visible mission control center in Part I. In Part II we looked at how it is structured and its components, giving you the opportunity to identify the elements that you already have. Perhaps you even drafted or created the elements that you needed quickly, so that you could start steering your organization.

In that case you will be starting with a mission control center that's already up and running, even if it's not complete. However, the goal of this book is not simply to help you complete your mission control center. Its goal is to enable you to be more successful at strategically managing your organization by better identifying your threats and opportunities, and reacting to them appropriately.

This chapter will provide you with an overview of the steps you need to take every time you develop your goal cycle. In subsequent chapters, we will be diving deeper into the visible mission process and activities.

SETTING UP YOUR GOALS

When we look at NASA's approach to getting to the Moon, we can imagine that they might have started with the vision (getting people to the Moon and back) and worked backwards. Figure 54 shows NASA's vision as an example of the starting point for a vision roadmap.

VISION ROADMAP		
	Time	**Time**
Lunar Landing	*Know Which Questions Find Answers*	Success

Figure 54 – NASA's vision

To get people to the Moon and back, NASA first needed to test getting equipment to and from the Moon. They then needed to test human orbit, human space flight, space flight, and a series of technical issues during the Apollo space program. Working backwards, they broke their vision down into the themes and phases illustrated in Figure 55.

VISION ROADMAP						
	Time	**Time**	**Time**	**Time**	**Time**	**Time**
Unscrewed Suborbital	*Know Which Questions Find Answers*					
Uncrewed Orbital		*Know Which Questions Find Answers*				
Crewed Orbital			*Know Which Questions Find Answers*			
Lunar Orbital				*Know Which Questions Find Answers*		
Lunar Landing					*Know Which Questions Find Answers*	Success

Figure 55 –Themes and phases necessary to achieve NASA's vision

The implementation looked like Figure 56, as NASA figured out what they could and should test with each of their missions.

APOLLO PROGRAM							
	1961-1963	1964	1965	1966	1967	1968	1969
	Mission(s)	Mission(s)	Mission(s)	Mission(s)	Mission(s)	Mission(s)	Mission(s)
Unscrewed Suborbital	*Oct 61 SA-1 Aprl 62 SA-2 Nov 62 SA-3 Mar 63 SA-4*			*Feb AS-201 Aug AS-202*			
Uncrewed Orbital		*Jan SA-5 May SA-7 Sep SA-7*	*Feb SA-9 May SA-8 Jul SA-10*	*Jul AS-203*	*Nov Apollo 4*	*Jan Apollo 5 Apr Apollo 6*	
Crewed Orbital						*Oct Apollo 7*	
Lunar Orbital						*Dec Apollo 8*	*Apr Apollo 9 May Apollo 10*
Lunar Landing							*Jul Apollo 11*

Figure 56 – Apollo space program mission timeline

As we can see from Figure 56, there were a series of missions to develop and test NASA's technologies, processes, etc. Each new mission built on what was learned on previous missions, until Apollo 11 landed successfully on the Sea of Tranquility in July 1969. The astronauts made it safely back to Earth four days later.

You can take the same approach as NASA did for your business. Start with your vision and work backwards to figure out what needs to be in place for your vision to become a reality. This will enable you to create your own vision roadmap. Figure 57 shows a vision roadmap for El Jefe.

VISION ROADMAP								
		Goal Cycles						
		Past-1	Past	Current	Next	Next+1	Next+n	Vision
THEME	**Truck & Test**	Clean Truck	Kitchen Setup Test Kitchen	**Miami Test Run**				
	Administr.			**Permits, etc. Finances**	*Permits Finances*	Permits	Permits	Permits
	Miami to LA				*New Orleans Austin*			
	Food Truck					The Brig Events	Events	
	Restaurant						Explore Options	Restaurant
	Other							

Figure 57 – El Jefe's vision roadmap

NASA uses the term 'mission' to describe a particular effort. I use the term 'Goal Cycle' (shown just under the 'Vision Roadmap' heading in Figure 57) for two reasons:

1) the purpose of your organization is to define and achieve its goals. The term 'Goal Cycle' will remind you of that. The goals of each of your cycles are milestones to achieve along the way as you realize your vision, just like NASA did with the Apollo space program.

2) a goal cycle can have a different frequency than other types of organizational reporting (such as annual financial reporting). For example, if you have a number of uncertainties when you enter a new market or introduce a new product, you may need to have goal cycles that span a month or a quarter, rather than a longer timeframe.

Putting your vision roadmap together informs you how to define your next goal cycle.

(If you are concerned that you don't have a complete vision roadmap right now: don't be. It develops as you start figuring out what you have, what you can achieve along the way, what you need to develop, etc. That's why the arrows in Figure 58 show that information flows in all directions, not just forward.)

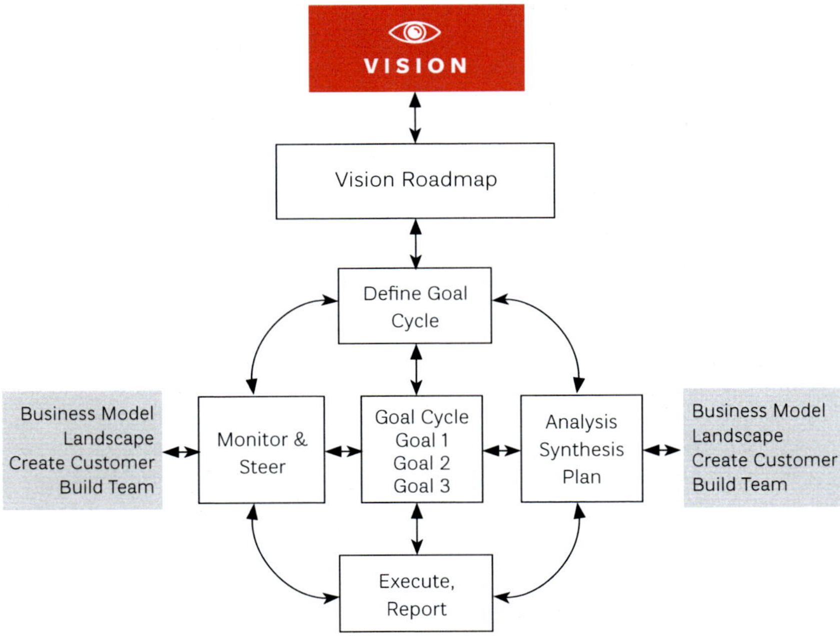

Figure 58 – Vision, vision roadmap, and goal cycle

As we have seen, NASA had a series of efforts[59] that they executed to move ever closer to the Moon landing. Each of the efforts were defined, analyzed, planned, executed, monitored and steered.

In the same way, your visible mission control center will help you to do the following:

---

59 Missions.

- define your goal (cycle)
- analyze and synthesize what you know (plan)
- execute your activities and report your progress
- monitor (your execution) and steer (adjusting as needed).

There could be a few interrelated goals for each of your goal cycles. Your plans are informed by the analytical activities that you will be doing through the different parts of your visible mission. Your analysis and planning cannot be separated. Your plans are captured in your goal cycles.

Your goal cycles (plans) will contain your 'Create Customer' and 'Build Team' goals. These plans will form the basis for your organization's execution of your activities. Reality emerges during the execution phase. The information you gather by monitoring your execution will give you a reality check on your progress and inform your steering. Your steering is the decisions you will make to navigate to the successful completion of each goal cycle.

PLANNING YOUR VISIBLE MISSION PROCESS FLOW

The process flow in developing your visible mission is reflected in Figure 59. It starts with your vision (the top row of the 'Vision and Progress' view) and progresses clockwise through the views: 'Blueprint and Landscape', 'Create Customer', and 'Build Team' before finishing with your progress (the bottom row of the 'Vision and Progress' view).

Within each view, there is usually a left-to-right, top-to-bottom flow.

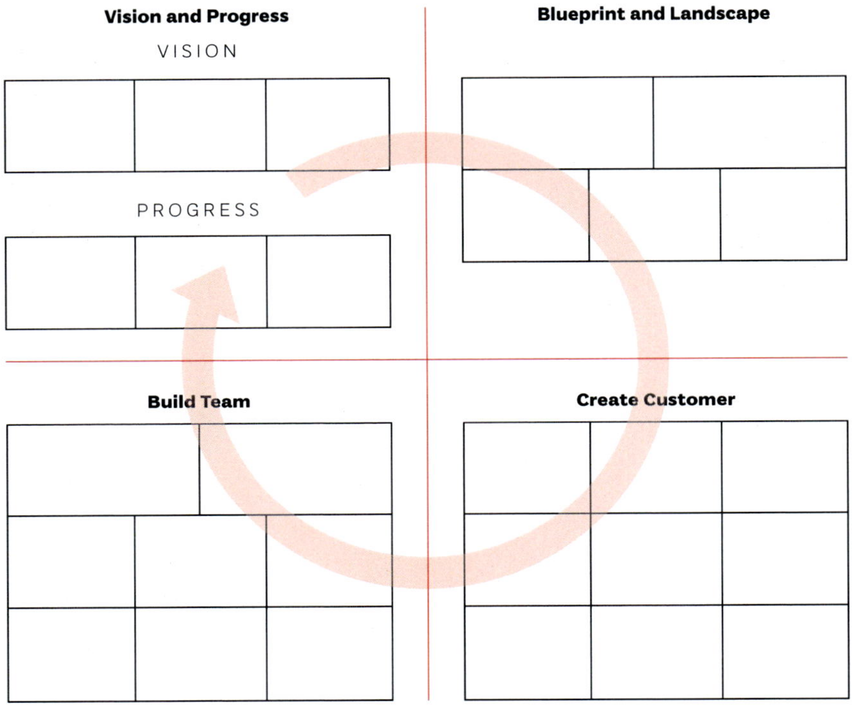

Figure 59 – Visible mission general flow

However, the visible mission is not a one-direction, single-pass, linear process: it is more like a conversation that is guided forward toward a unified and coordinated plan. Let's look at its conversational flow.

ENSURING YOUR VISIBLE MISSION CONVERSATION FLOW

The elements that you are working on at any given time in your visible mission control center are generally dependent on (or informed by) your previous elements and preceding views.

For example, your 'Create Customer' work needs to uncover customer, product and market solutions to reflect your vision and your business model. However, during your customer empathy and product work, you may discover that your original vision and business model assumptions (such as key resources and value streams) are wrong. These incorrect assumptions may be constraining your 'Create Customer' initiatives. Insights like these may require you to update your business model to reflect newly uncovered realities. You might even have to reconsider your vision!

Similarly, when you get to the 'Build Team' analysis of your key resources and value streams, you may realize that the capabilities you require are not feasible to develop during the goal cycle. You may then have to reconsider your business model and your 'Create Customer' efforts in terms of what is feasible and affordable during this goal cycle.

Figure 60 illustrates that the visible mission is not a linear progression, but rather a way to work through and come up with:

1) the best goals for your organization, and

2) the best plans to achieve those goals.

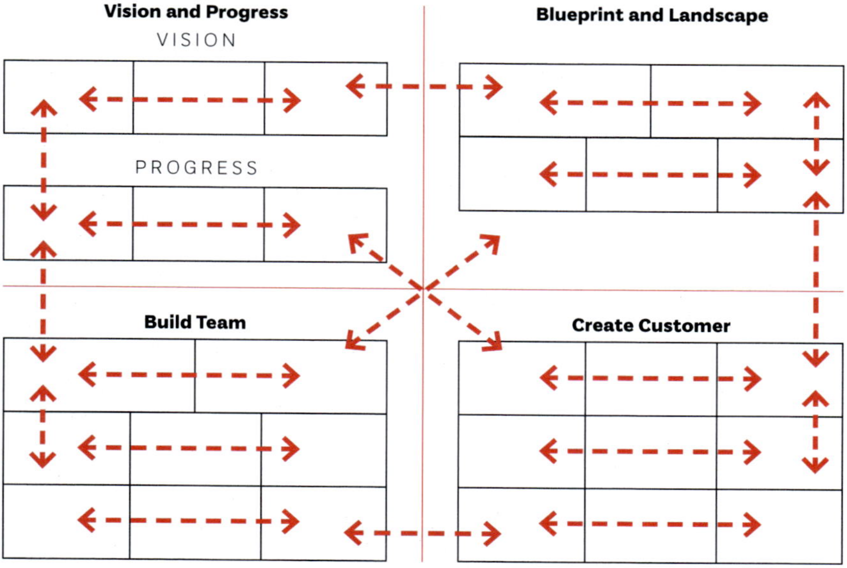

Figure 60 – Visible mission conversation flow

The way to have this conversation flow when using your visible mission is to do a reality check as you move forward. Regularly look back at each of your views and ask the following question:

- is the view information still true, accurate and real, or do you need to change it now that we know more, or now that we know better?

Doing this creates a working visible mission model with the integrity to empower you to make better and more informed decisions.

With that said, let's get into the exciting part of the strategy!

TO DO

Schedule your planning, executing, monitoring and steering activities (that need to be developed and agreed upon for your upcoming goal cycle). Below is a sample schedule.

- Introduction meeting explaining the visible mission process flow to your team.
- A half-day each spent on compiling your 'Vision and Mission', and 'Blueprint and Landscape' views.
- A whole day for the 'Create Customer' view.
- A whole day for the 'Build Team' view.
- A half-day for the coordination of your visible mission goals, metrics and initiatives.

You should then schedule your monitoring sessions.

The times proposed are guidelines. For example, if you really want to dig into your mission, then you can schedule a day-long, off-site working session for that.

You get the point.

> **Your vision is achieved through achieving a series of goals that are implemented in goal cycles. Each cycle consists of analysis, goal-setting, planning, executing, monitoring, and adjustment.**

Although there is a general flow, the planning and execution of your visible mission is not a linear process. It is a guided conversation that lets you develop realistic and inspiring goals, metrics and initiatives. This is the basis of incrementally building the world that is described in your vision.

Using your visible mission to plan and execute creates a structured way of seeing your interdependencies. It allows you to place relevant events into context quicker, and to understand and communicate their implications faster. This also enables you to react faster and with more confidence.

NASA achieved the vision of the Moon landing through a series of missions. In this chapter, we saw what their vision roadmap might have looked like, and how they ended up executing their roadmap. Each mission was planned based on what was known, and had a clear goal and plan to achieve the goal. Their plans were executed, progress was monitored and necessary adjustments were made. NASA knew when to adapt, and sometimes, even when to abort goals. The Mission Control Center framework they used enabled them to understand and contextualize new data very quickly, so that they could react not only appropriately, but quickly as well.

With the concept of the series of goal cycles in your visible mission now established, let's dive deeper into the first (and very important) part of the process flow – reviewing the vision section of your 'Vision and Progress' view.

CHAPTER 13

Digging Deeper into Your Vision, Mission, Goal Cycles and Assumptions

NASA did not have to come up with a vision, it was given to them. But as far as visions go, it was a glowing example of the power of a great vision. It can inspire us as a species to achieve almost unimaginable things. NASA's vision not only created a goal, it also focused the attention and resources of many people.

Similarly, the purpose of developing a vision for your organization is not because 'everybody does'. It is so you can inspire and lead your team to achieve great things.

In the previous chapter, we saw how NASA's vision roadmap was broken down into multiple missions. Our equivalent of NASA's missions are goal cycles.

> **A vision is the common purpose for your plans and the work contained in those plans. It is your North Star that you should use to navigate. Without a goal you will be moving without ever really getting anywhere, just like Alice in Wonderland.**
>
> **However, having a vision is not enough. You need a way to realize your vision. The goal cycle in the visible mission helps you to achieve your vision. At the end of each goal cycle, you should have moved closer to achieving your vision.**

Your goal cycles will be based on assumptions that you need to make obvious and manage appropriately

You need to do this repeatedly as you build your organization's vision.

You are here.

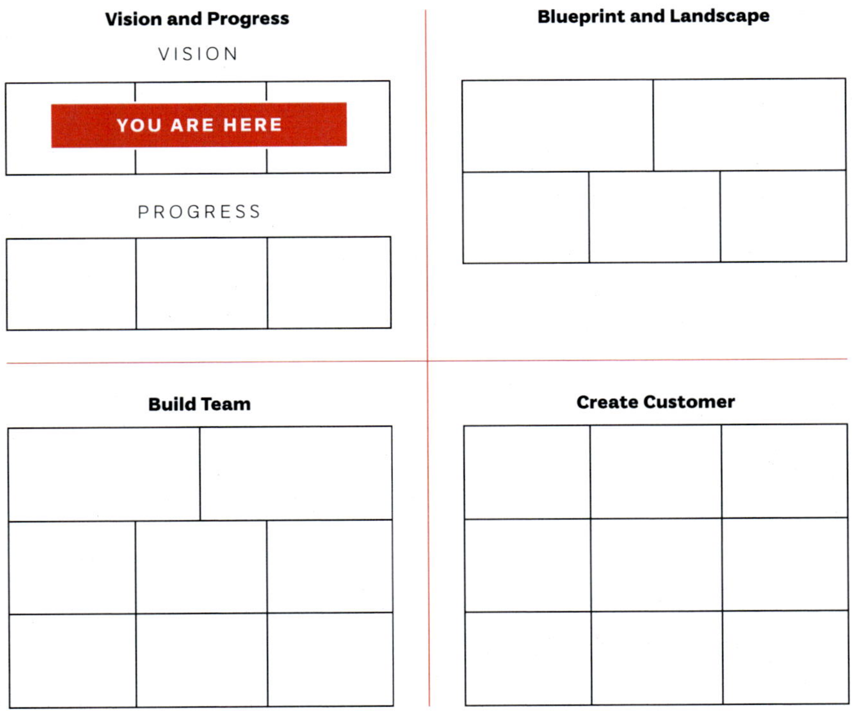

Figure 61 – You are here

REVIEWING YOUR VISION AND MISSION

Your vision is the anchoring point for your organization. It functions as your North Star to help you navigate. Recall from Chapter 5 that your vision is what you and your team are working on building. Your mission on the other hand describes the 'how' – or more specifically, what you will be doing to realize your vision.

Ideally, you should review and confirm your vision and mission annually, because there will be a range of possibilities with each goal cycle, with each project, and with every change in circumstances that may require one or both to be adjusted.

Vision and Mission Workshop

Purpose/Output: vision and mission confirmation or re-draft.

Suggested duration: 1 hour (review), 4 hours (initial draft).

Frequency: in theory, once in a lifetime, but good to review/confirm annually.

Participants: your leadership team.

Additional resources: search 'best vision and mission examples' online (and refer back to Figure 11 in Chapter 5 to review El Jefe's vision and mission).

REVIEWING YOUR GOAL CYCLES

In the previous chapter, we have looked at how goal cycles are used to work toward the vision.

VISION ROADMAP								
		Goal Cycles						
		Past-1	Past	Current	Next	Next+1	Next+n	Vision
THEME	**Truck & Test**	Clean Truck	Kitchen Setup Test Kitchen	**Miami Test Run**				
	Administr.			**Permits, etc. Finances**	*Permits Finances*	Permits	Permits	Permits
	Miami to LA				*New Orleans Austin*			
	Food Truck					The Brig Events	Events	
	Restaurant						Explore Options	Restaurant
	Other							

Figure 62 – El Jefe goal cycles

In the example in Figure 62 for El Jefe, the 'Past', 'Current', 'Next' and 'Vision' column headings provide general goal cycle structures that you can use. Each column represents a planning horizon, and has a particular focus and function. The 'Vision' column is critical, since it keeps your eyes on the big picture, and helps you to develop the steps along the way (your vision roadmap).

The 'Current' goal cycle is important for keeping your focus on your current work and preventing scope creep. It is used to identify visible, incremental steps towards your vision.

The planning of the 'Next' goal cycle is done towards the end of the current, active goal cycle that you are working on. If your timing is great, your 'Next' cycle will be planned and ready to become your new 'Current' goal cycle as soon as the 'Current' one becomes 'Past'.

The 'Next' goal cycle will contain the next set of goals that will again take you closer to achieving your vision. During the planning process, you will determine exactly what ends up in your 'Next' goal cycle. Once your 'Next' goes cycle becomes your 'Current' one, you can create another upcoming goal cycle that will become the new 'Next' one.

Figure 63 shows this transition for the goal cycles from Figure 62.

VISION ROADMAP								
		Goal Cycles						
		Past-2	Past-1	Past	Current	Next	Next+n	Vision
THEME	**Truck & Test**	Clean Truck	Kitchen Setup Test Kitchen	Miami Test Run				
	Administr.			Permits, etc. Finances	**Permits Finances**	*Permits*	Permits	Permits
	Miami to LA				**New Orleans Austin**			
	Food Truck					*The Brig Events*	Events	
	Restaurant						Explore Options	Restaurant
	Other							

Figure 63 – El Jefe goal cycle transition

Goal Cycles Workshop

Purpose/Output: Define your upcoming and subsequent goal cycles, including aspirational goals.

Next goal cycle questions to answer:

- what do we need or want to achieve?
- what goals are we defining?
- do the goals move us closer to our vision?
- are there goals that we want to put in the subsequent (later) goal cycle? (These may be goals for which we are not ready to achieve yet.)

Suggested duration: 1 hour.

Frequency: depends on the duration of your goal cycles. It is typically done annually. Adjust as needed.

Participants: your leadership team.

The goals that you place in your 'Next' goal cycle will form the basis of your planning, but depending on what you find, they may be adjusted. For example, if the goals are too optimistic or too conservative, they should be adjusted as you proceed with your analysis and planning.

You can use any of the later goal cycles as 'parking lots' for ideas or aspirational goals. If there are goals in any of your parking lots that have expired, delete them, and if there are new, relevant ones, add them. Some of the goals in your later cycles may lose meaning if there is a shift in your focus.

At this point, your goals can be in a draft state, and the detail other than a name and a short description is negotiable. Do add a (short) description – what is very obvious to the person coming up with the goal may not be that obvious to someone else (or even the same person a month or two later).

REVIEWING YOUR ASSUMPTIONS

Goal cycles obviously rest on a number of critical assumptions.
One of my customers once said, "All of planning is an assumption", and that is true to some extent. Having your critical assumptions in such a prominent place in your visible mission is a reminder to not be blindsided by your assumptions if they turn out to be wrong. It also helps to keep you humble and honest with yourself.

Let's be honest, every time we come up with an idea for a product that will be the next big thing, we can't imagine that it won't succeed. Everybody needs this! The world will love it! This is based on a few basic assumptions:

- there is a need;
- there is enough of a need for enough people to have a market

large enough to succeed;

- our product solves the need (or the problem) better than any other solution; and
- that our solution can be accessed by our intended market.

Assumptions work a lot better with some humility. You should test all the critical assumptions that your business model, product, marketing, production, distribution and support are based on.

The assumption matrix helps you to make uncertain assumptions more certain as quickly as possible. Recall from Chapter 5 that the matrix shows your assumptions on a grid with two axes: *criticality* and *uncertainty*. The more your success depends on the certainty of your assumption, the more critical that assumption is.

Let's say I assume that my product solution meets my customers' needs. If it doesn't, then I have no business. That qualifies as a *critical* assumption.

The *uncertainty* is whether I know anything about the likelihood of the assumption being true (or false). If I have it only in my head, the uncertainty is very high. If I have some research, or comparative solutions, then the uncertainty reduces somewhat. It is only when I have customers using the product that the uncertainty is reduced significantly.

Assumptions Workshop

Purpose/Output: identify critical assumptions, create a directory, and produce an assumption matrix.

Suggested duration*:* 1 hour.

Frequency*:* as needed, at least during goal cycle planning.

Participants*:* leadership team.

Additional Resources: *UX for Lean Startups: Faster, Smarter User Experience Research and Design,* by Laura Klein.[60]

---

60 *UX for Lean Startups: Faster, Smarter User Experience Research and Design* by Laura Klein (2018), O'Reilly Media.

TO DO

- Each person creates a list of assumptions (sticky notes are recommended).
- Review the existing assumptions, and update as needed (if test, research, or other data is available). Add the new assumptions by going around the table to add or update.
- Rate each assumption in terms of criticality and uncertainty. (Use a 5-point scale).
- Assumption tests: Is it testable? Draft a test plan with a target date, and assign it.
- Draft an assumption matrix along the criticality and uncertainty axes. (You can also use a large sheet or a whiteboard with sticky notes to place your assumptions.)

Figure 64 shows a compiled assumption list for El Jefe. Figure 65 shows that information on an assumption matrix.

Name	Description	Criticality (1-5)	Uncertainty (1-5)	Test
Truck viable	Assuming the truck will be able to reliably travel around. (It is very critical since this way one can attend events, or high-traffic areas. The truck is new, and appeared to be in bad shape, so the uncertainty is high.)	4	4	Get the truck to an auto mechanic for a through service, and figure out how to do basic maintenance and trouble-shooting.
Permits	Assuming the permits will be easy-enough the get, and affordable. (Highly critical since without a permit, no sales are permitted. Uncertainty is medium, since Carl has experience with regular restaurant permits.)	5	2	Visit city-hall and figure out how to do.
Cuisine	Assume the food, the quality ingredients, the regional and seasonal approach will attract the right attention. Highly critical, since this is the heart of the vision, and uncertainty is low beacuse it has worked before.	5	1	Cook, and see how people react.

Figure 64 – El Jefe assumption list

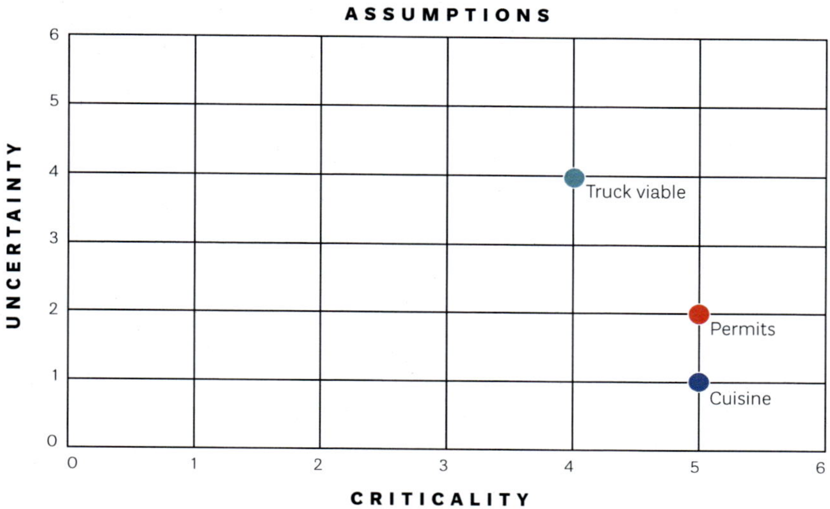

Figure 65 – El Jefe assumption matrix

> **Your vision anchors everything that you do with the development of your goal cycles. It determines your business model, your competitive landscape, how you create your customers, and how you develop your team.**
>
> **As you define your goal cycles, you make sure that you have those things in your planning cycle that are absolutely necessary, nothing less. Take your assumptions seriously – even if you acknowledge that an assumption cannot be tested. Whenever possible, test your assumptions as quickly and as cheaply as possible.**

The vision of the Moon landing has not only inspired the people working on the Apollo space program, it is still an inspiration. It is a testament to:

- what people can achieve when bound and inspired by a common purpose,

- what people can do when we focus our energies and abilities, and
- how we can proceed even under great stress and uncertainty. Even when we fail along the way.

We can and should do the same with our organizations. We not only have the opportunity, we also have a responsibility to make the world a better place – for us, our children, our society, and for the planet.

With your North Star visible on the 'Vision' view of your visible mission (and firmly settled in your mind), hopefully you and your team are energized by your vision. It clarifies what you are setting out to achieve.

Once you have reviewed your vision, mission, goal cycles and assumption matrix, you are ready to dig deeper into your 'Blueprint and Landscape' view in Chapter 14. This view is your 'spacecraft' and the environment you need to navigate. We will look further at your business model, industry assessment, blue ocean strategy, and emerging future.

CHAPTER 14

Digging Deeper into Your Blueprint and Landscape

As we saw in chapter 6, in order to succeed, NASA had to understand the environment that their astronauts had to travel through and survive. They had to build a vehicle that could travel to the Moon and back without endangering the lives of the astronauts.

NASA had to figure out what environmental factors were critical to the success of their missions, how to interpret them, and how to react appropriately. They needed to have an eye on the environment, e.g. the weather, temperatures, solar activity, etc. If necessary, they had to make changes to their plans, and even to their missions.

They also had to keep a close eye on how the spacecraft and its different parts were doing. For example, during take-off: did the rocket function appropriately, did the separations function properly? During space flight: is the craft functioning properly, and are the conditions in the craft within the operating parameters, etc. (e.g. the oxygen 'scrubber' needed to function properly to ensure the astronauts could breathe).

How can you design and monitor the right 'spacecraft' (i.e. the right business model) for your purpose? What are the pieces that make up your environment? How can you monitor your environment to provide you with the best possible view to avoid unnecessary risks, deal with those you can't avoid, and identify and maximize opportunities?

Your business model allows you to make your structure clear. It also creates agreement on critical aspects like your customers, value propositions, key activities, how you make money, and what your expenses will be.

The visible mission's tools enable you to explore different business models to survive in a changing environment, and to create competitive advantage opportunities.

You collect and share information, and learn about your business environment by using the visible mission's landscape tools. They include your industry assessment, your emerging future and your blue ocean strategy.

Your business blueprint and landscape provide the context for the creation of your customers, and the building of the organization you need to succeed.

You are here.

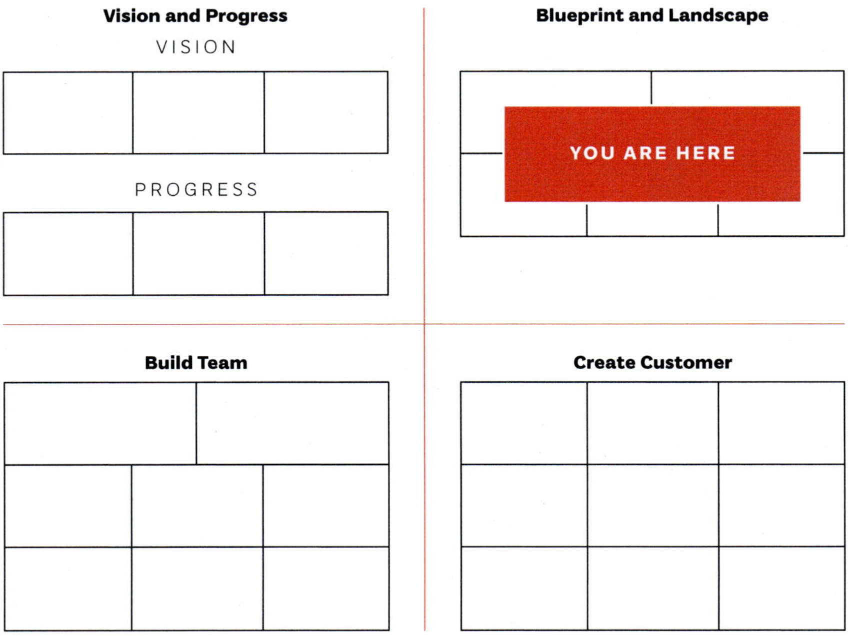

Figure 66 – You are here

There are visual 'shorthand' representations of all of the elements of the 'Blueprint and Landscape' view of the visible mission. These visuals make the 'Blueprint and Landscape' view very easy to understand and communicate, even though there is lots of detail behind them. Both the visualizations and the detail are integral to your success. The visualizations speed up the understanding and communication of key information, while the detail provides critical context and insights. Together they form a killer combination.

REVIEWING YOUR BLUEPRINT SECTION

As you know from Chapter 6, the blueprint section of your visible mission helps you to look at your organization, much like an MRI scan provides a high-resolution representation of our bodies. The business model views are particularly useful to show:

1) how you intend to (or are) making money, and

2) how your organization currently shapes up in terms of customers and products, as well as what you need to do to deliver the right product at the right time to solve your customers' needs.

This is the organization that you have (and/or need to have) to help you succeed.

Using the Business Model Navigator

As outlined in Chapter 6, the Business Model Navigator helps you to consider:

- what you offer your customers,
- who your customers are,
- how your value proposition is created, and
- why you generate profit.

If you are an already running business, you might wonder why you should bother with using it in your visible mission.

However, for all the discussions about the need for innovation to succeed in business, the need for business model innovation is likely to be the most powerful one. Many of the major shifts that we have seen in business success in recent decades relate to innovation at the business model level. For example, Amazon moved from in-store to digital shopping, complete with warehousing and logistics. Similarly, with Netflix you are still watching a movie (the same product), but instead of picking it up somewhere like the now defunct Blockbuster retail chain, you are streaming it online due to Netflix innovating with their business model.

Of course, some of these shifts are enabled by technologies, but Netflix created a new business model even before anyone could stream. They delivered rental DVDs to consumers.

The authors of the Business Model Navigator have identified 55 business model types, or combinations, that most businesses use to succeed. The Business Model Navigator is a great resource to explore business models (like digitization, self-help, etc.) that you may be able to use to exploit new opportunities.

Figure 67 shows a description of El Jefe's business model using the Business Model Navigator.

What (do you offer the customer?)
Restaurant quality food from a food truck, at events, "happenings"
Who (is your target customer?)
Event attendees, wanting awesome food
How (is your value proposition created?)
Great local, seasonal ingredients Restaurant level cooking experience Dependable staff Strong social media presences
Why (does this business model generate a profit?)
Can sell the food at a premium Established, and growing customer base Dependable, high quality food
Business Model Pattern
Experience Selling

Mission Control-Toolbox
Business Model Navigator, 2014, Grassman, Frankenberger, Csik

Figure 67 – Business Model Navigator detail (El Jefe)

Business Model Navigator Workshop

Purpose/Output: describe your current business model and/or examine other potential business models.

Suggest duration: A draft can be done in an hour. You can continue to enrich, and refine as needed.

Frequency: You could dig into your business model evaluation when you do your goal cycle planning, or when you are experiencing competitive or industry pressures. You can do it internally with your own team (customer service, product development, sales and marketing) to look at your alternatives. It can be done as a single workshop, or if you want to get into more detail, a series of workshops.

I recommend that you start off by analyzing what your business model is when you start out (or when you started out). Also set time aside to explore other options. You can probably do that on the back of an envelope over a couple of hours.

Participants: your leadership, customer service, product development, sales and marketing teams.

Additional Resources: Apart from the book, there are also consulting services available associated with the Business Model Navigator team.

Using the Business Model Canvas

As outlined in Chapter 6, the Business Model Canvas is another visual representation of your business. It uses nine building blocks that make up all businesses and organizations. This structure holds true for groups like departments and teams within larger organizations (including not-for-profit and government organizations).

The Business Model Canvas is a great tool to describe your organization and to get everyone on the same page. Figure 68 provides a blank template you can use.

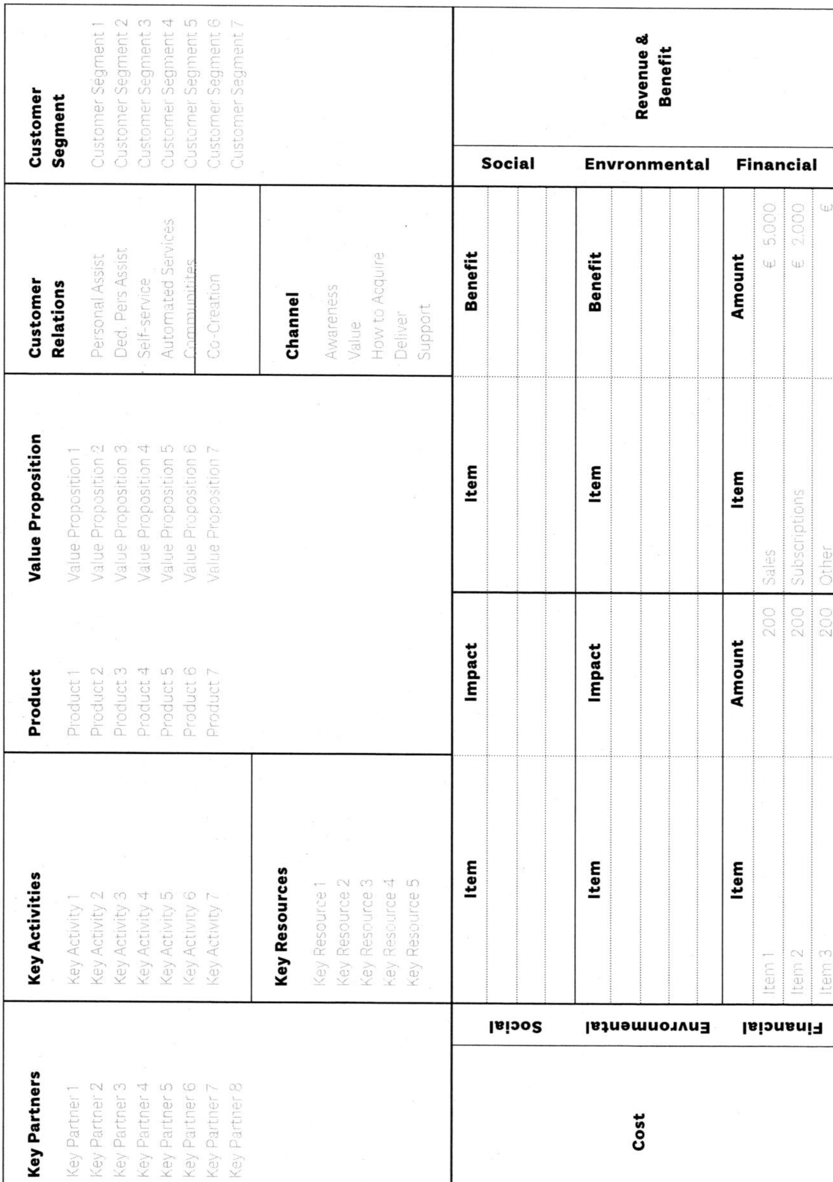

Figure 68 – Business Model Canvas template

The most frequent response I have received from teams using the Canvas is "My goodness, I didn't know that we're doing all of this!"[61] That's because people tend to only be familiar with their own part of an organization. They usually have some idea of what's happening elsewhere, based partly on fact, assumption and imagination. It's only when the parts of the organization are brought together and made visible to all that everyone gets closer to its true picture. It's rare that anybody in an organization (including its leaders) has a clear view.

Using the Business Model Canvas allows you to bring all your assumptions and all of the things you imagine you know about your organization to the forefront, and replace them if necessary with facts. I can almost guarantee that there will be different ideas on what various elements on your Canvas mean. When this happens, it's a great opportunity to bring those differences out in the open. They will not be new differences – they will simply have existed 'safely' in isolation in the minds of your team members. They might have even caused some confusion and conflicting decisions in your organization in the past.

For example, if one person assumes that your customer relationships are mostly driven towards a self-help approach, and another person thinks that you would do a lot better by focusing on personal assistance, then these conflicts can be resolved when they are out in the open. It may be that both are right for slightly different customer segments. These differences can be clearly defined, understood or communicated. Having a conversation with a colleague about a channel problem using the Business Model Canvas makes it easier to visualize the customer segment and the product/value proposition. It becomes a lot easier to include the resources and activities involved in establishing a successful channel to each customer segment.

---

61 A variation of the Business Model Canvas that I use includes 'Environmental' and 'Social' measures on both the 'Revenue' and 'Cost' sides. It enables you to look at non-financial measures that may be critical for you to achieve, e.g. CO2-positive and water on the environmental side, and diversity, gender and race on the social side.

Knowing the parts of your organization and understanding how they relate to each other will make it easier for you to develop and steer it. The Canvas helps to encourage far better communication about what is happening in the organization, and what should be happening.

The Business Model Canvas also provides a very general reference for the 'Create Customer' and 'Build Team' parts of your visible mission. Figure 69 shows how the views are related to elements on the Canvas.

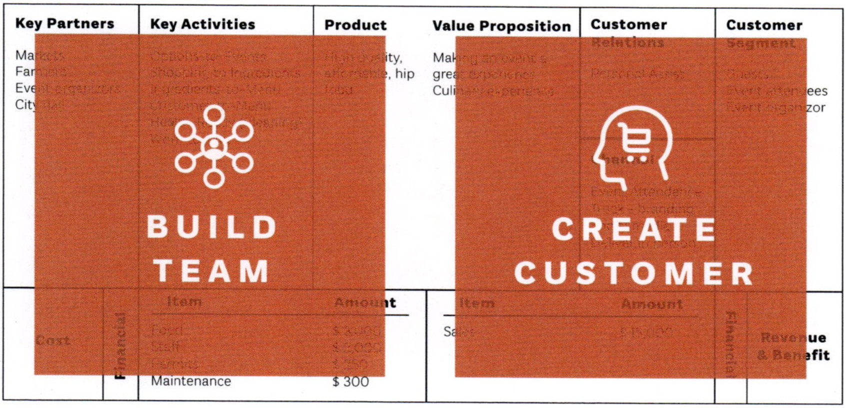

Figure 69 – 'Create Customer' and 'Build Team' views as they relate to the Business Model Canvas

Business Model Canvas Workshop

Purpose/Outcome: develop an easy-to-understand and easy-to-communicate description of your business to guide your exploration of problems and opportunities, encourage collaboration, etc.

Suggested duration: a solid draft can be done in an hour. Another hour can get you additional detail on each of the elements, e.g. customer segments, value propositions, etc.

Frequency: I recommend drafting a first version as soon as possible. You should be able to do this in a few minutes. I also recommend you do this with your leadership team as part of planning your goal cycles. A workshop is a good place to do it.

Participants: your leadership team.

Additional resources: *Business Model Generation* by Osterwalder and Pigneur does a great job describing how you can do this. [62]

An online search will also point you to consultants if you want outside help.

REVIEWING YOUR LANDSCAPE SECTION

As you know from Chapter 6, the landscape section of your visible mission provides a view of your environment: think of it like a radar image. There are three tools you can use in your landscape section: industry assessment, emerging future, and blue ocean strategy.

These tools will help you to keep an eye on your environment, and enable you to quickly understand:

- what environmental events relate to your organization, and
- whether you need to do anything about an event (and if so, how you should respond).

For example, you may see changes in a traditional competitor and understand that they are trying a different business model. This information is useful to know.

Industry Assessment

Your industry assessment enables you to develop an overall view of the 'players' in your industry: customers, suppliers and partners, traditional competitors, new competitors, and replacement products.

Even mature industries are exposed to change, and sometimes to sudden change. It's always good to keep an eye on what's happening in your industry. You need to look in the right places, and ask the right questions. Figure 70 provides a template you can use.

---

62 *Business Model Generation*, Osterwalder and Pigneur (2010), Wiley.

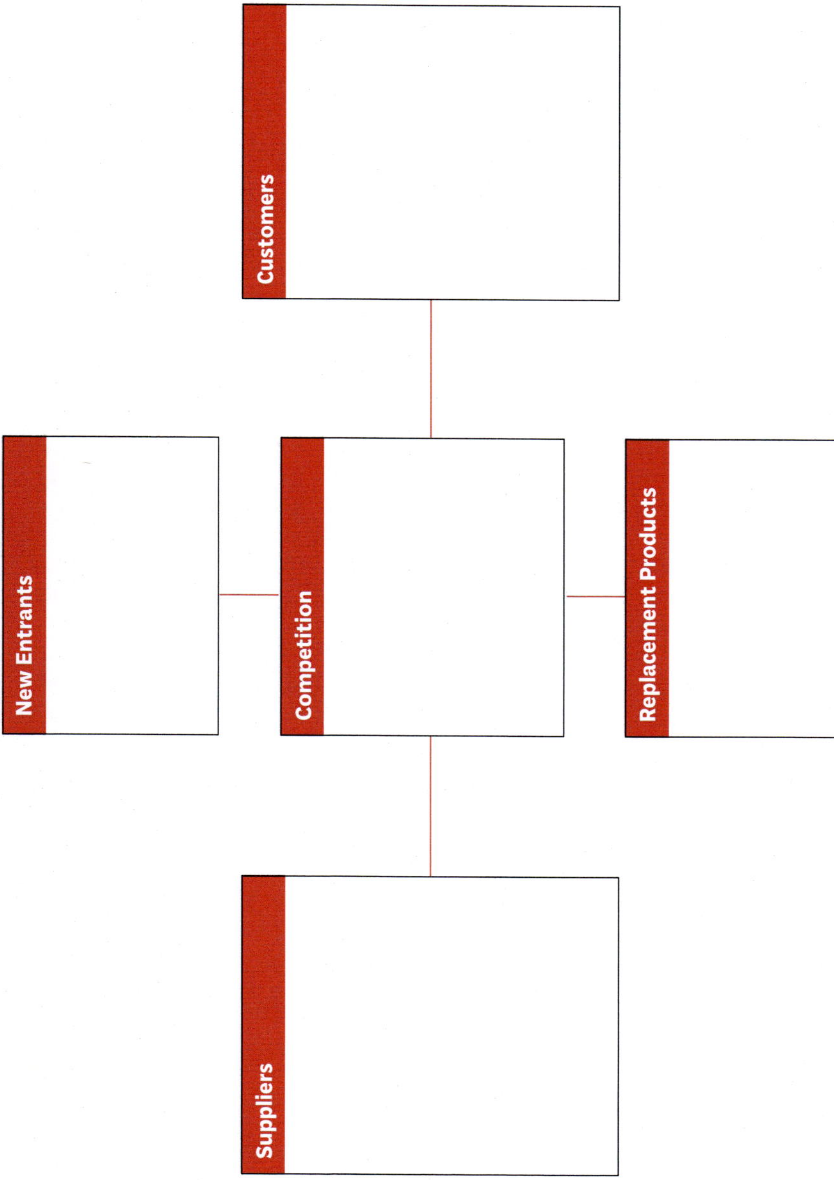

Figure 70 – Five forces industry assessment template

Industry Assessment Workshop

Purpose/Outcome: understand what your industry forces are, and whether they are positive or negative in terms of how they affect your organization. Develop insights to inform your options and decisions.

Suggested duration: review – 1 hour, deep dive – workshop for necessary time. (You need a deep dive if you've never done an industry assessment before or if you sense that there are things influencing your industry but you can't place your finger on those things.)

Frequency: it could be ongoing, or at least during your goal cycle planning sessions.

Participants: your leadership team.

Emerging Future

As outlined in Chapter 6, the emerging future section of your visible mission uses the PESTLE tool. It enables you to look for major trends relevant to your success. These trends could be related to:

- **politics** (local, national or international) – e.g. "America First", "New Green Deal", etc.
- the **environment** – e.g. CO_2, fossil-fuel or regenerative power generation, 'Fridays for Future', etc.
- **society** – e.g. migration, the shrinking middle-class, COVID-19, conspiracy theories, etc.
- **technology** – e.g. digitization, miniaturization, IoT, etc.
- the **law** (local, national or international) – e.g. tax laws, Brexit, anti-competition, data privacy, etc.
- **economic** conditions (local, national or international).

Figure 71 provides a template you can use for your PESTLE trend identification.

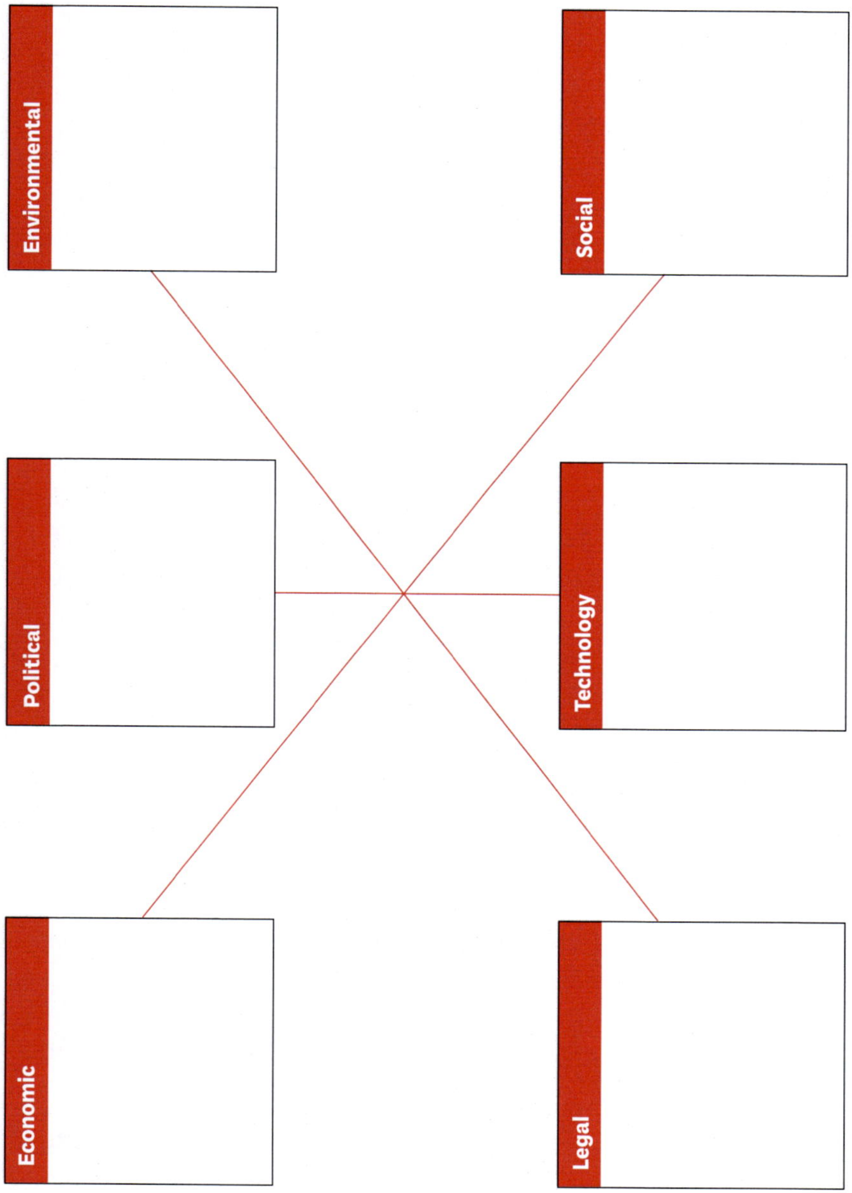

Figure 71 – PESTLE trend identification template

Using the PESTLE tool allows you to see whether trends represent a future opportunity or a threat. For example:

- do you have the opportunity to move your product/service as a digital and/or online solution?
- are your products and services at risk of being replaced by a digital or online solution?
- is your market disappearing due to demographic and cultural changes (e.g. Harley-Davidson)? It also enables you to assess the capabilities you have in relation to the trends, as well as identify the capabilities you may need.

Emerging Future Workshop

Purpose/Output: understanding major trends that will impact your business, customers, etc. The trends in your PESTLE should be supported by a more detailed description of their anticipated effects on your organization.

Suggested duration: preparation – 1 hour: group and rate the items in three buckets: current, near-term, and long-term. Near-term and long-term may mean different time frames in different industries. Decide what time frames work best for you based on when you need to take action to respond to the trend: during this goal cycle, during the next, or whether you won't take any action but will keep an eye on the trend.

Frequency: this PESTLE analysis should be done at least during your goal cycle planning, but keep a constant eye on trends and emerging trends. It may be that some events are not part of a trend, or that the trend is far more drawn out than expected (e.g. self-driving cars).

Participants: your leadership team. You could also ask your team to keep their eyes open for trends. You can use the template in Figure 74 for a deeper analysis of each PESTLE trend you have identified.

Trend Name:
PESTLE Name:
Trend Description
Impact
Options

Figure 72 – PESTLE trend analysis template

Blue Ocean Strategy

As outlined in Chapter 6, the 'blue ocean strategy' is a great tool to help you understand your customers, non-customers and competition, as well as to help you find uncontested markets. The uncontested (or 'blue ocean') markets stand in contrast to highly competitive 'red ocean' markets. (The latter are metaphorically red to indicate the blood of your competitors.)

The blue ocean strategy tool could also help you identify when one of your competitors is developing a new, uncontested market. Knowing that information may help you to react faster.

Finding a blue ocean market starts with identifying critical customer factors, such as:

- what do they want more of?
- what do they want less of?
- what do they want eliminated?
- what do they want that's not available at the moment? (Of course, they don't necessarily need to be able to tell you: your innovative solutions may be exactly what they had been waiting for.)

Using your critical customer factors, you can rate your solution, and those of your competitors to create a strategy curve for an uncontested market. Figures 73 to 75 show how El Jefe could create a blue ocean strategy curve.

Eliminate	**Raise**
Barrier to customer	Accessibility (to all)
	Quality
	Regionality
	Seasoanlity
Reduce	**Create**
Stuffiness	5-star quality

Figure 73 – Critical customer factors (El Jefe)

Current Factors in Market (incl. own product)	El Jefe (Chef)	Trucks	Restaurants	Delivery	Concession Stands
Price	7	7	1	5	10
Food quality	9	7	10	4	3
Accessibility	10	10	7	7	10
Customer access	10	10	2	2	4
Atmosphere	10	10	7	1	1
Experience	10	10	7	3	2

Figure 74 – El Jefe's 'blue ocean' assessment

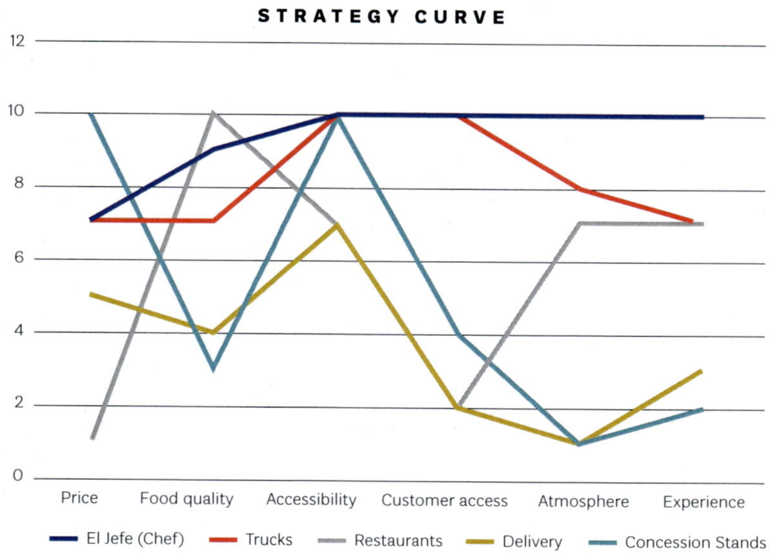

Figure 75 – Blue ocean strategy (El Jefe)

Blue Ocean Strategy Workshop

Purpose/Outcome: identify a potential blue ocean market.

Suggested duration: 1-hour preparation time per person, and 1 hour for the meeting. Deep dive as needed. (You need a deep dive if you've never done a blue ocean strategy session before, or if you are sensing that there are other solutions or value propositions that are crowding out your product/service, but you can't figure out exactly what is going on.)

Frequency: as needed, or during your goal cycle planning sessions.

Participants: your leadership team.

Additional resources: *Blue Ocean Strategy* by Kim and Mauborgne.[63]

Various consultants also specialize in helping businesses conduct blue ocean strategy sessions if you want outside help.

FOLLOW-UP WORK

If there is subsequent work coming out of your review of your 'Blueprint and Landscape' view, then add it as a goal to the relevant effort area (i.e. your 'Create Customer' or 'Build Team' views).

For example, if there are changes that will (or might) affect your customers, products, markets, etc., then it may be sensible to define goals, metrics and initiatives that will go on your 'Create Customer' roadmap. I

Or if there are changes or additional research is needed to review your business model value streams, or capabilities, then add it to your 'Build Team' roadmap.

But it's more important to identify the right work, rather than worry about which roadmap it should go on.

You need the right organization to succeed. Your success depends on your goals and your environment. Now you know what to prepare for.

> **Your business blueprint is a representation of your team and the organization you have that enables you to create customers.**

63 *Blue Ocean Strategy,* Kim and Mauborgne (2005), Harvard Business Review Press.

Your industry assessment gives you a view into your immediate competitive realities. Your emerging future shows you opportunities and threats, as well as ways to prepare and participate in shaping the future. Your blue ocean strategy can allow you to lead the way in uncontested markets.

NASA's spacecraft in the Apollo program had to be able to survive and operate in new and extreme conditions. In order to build their spacecraft, NASA had to understand what they needed to be able to endure. NASA first had to explore and understand the conditions their spacecraft would face.

This information was critical during the spacecraft's design and testing, but even more important during each mission's execution. The ability to track the information enabled NASA's Mission Control Center to adjust their missions, keep crews safe, and ultimately played a major role in accomplishing their Moon landing vision.

In addition to digging deeper into your vision and mission, goal cycles and assumptions from the previous chapter, this chapter has enabled you to get a clearer and more comprehensive shared view of your:

- organization and business model,
- industry,
- product/service's competitive profile, and
- emerging trends.

You can use this information to provide you with rich context when looking at your customers, their needs, and what you can do to help them. In chapter 15, you will be analyzing and planning how to both retain existing customers and create new ones by providing them with solutions that they need and value. You will figure out how to thrive in your environment by using what you know.

CHAPTER 15

Digging Deeper into Creating Customers: the Core of Strategy

Although the Moon landing was NASA's vision, there were a series of missions and a series of interim goals that had to be reached before the vision could be achieved. For example, there were satellites placed into space, the first person launched into space, the first into orbit, the first unmanned Moon mission, and finally the Moon landing.

There were answers to critical questions needed at each stage before it was possible for NASA to move to the next stage. Before they could test human space flight, they first needed to see if they could get a spacecraft into space and back, and be able to recover it. In order to do that, they needed to test whether a rocket could get it there. Before they could do that, they needed to be able to build and design a rocket, and a launch pad. And so on. As you saw from the vision roadmap in Chapter 12, NASA's vision development happened by focus area.

Similarly, with each mission (goal cycle) in your visible mission, you need to get the right balance. You don't want to stretch too far and endanger your progress. However, if you don't stretch far enough, you may simply repeat what you've done, and not gain anything from it. This will waste time, energy and resources.

As an organization, how should you decide what to do first to achieve your ultimate goal? What can you do? What should you do?

What is the best next thing to do? How do you take a critical look at your situation to determine and consider your options? What do you need in place to succeed?

Of course, our primary goal from a business perspective is to create and keep customers. We do this by providing them with solutions to a particular problem that's important to them.

Strategy is the set of choices of which customers to engage with (and under what circumstances).

You have to know and understand your customer and their problems. Your ability to empathize with your customers is critical to your ability to create innovative and valuable solutions.

You need to examine market opportunities. When you compare opportunities and your organization's ability to exploit them, you can choose which customers to engage with (and when to engage with them).

You are here.

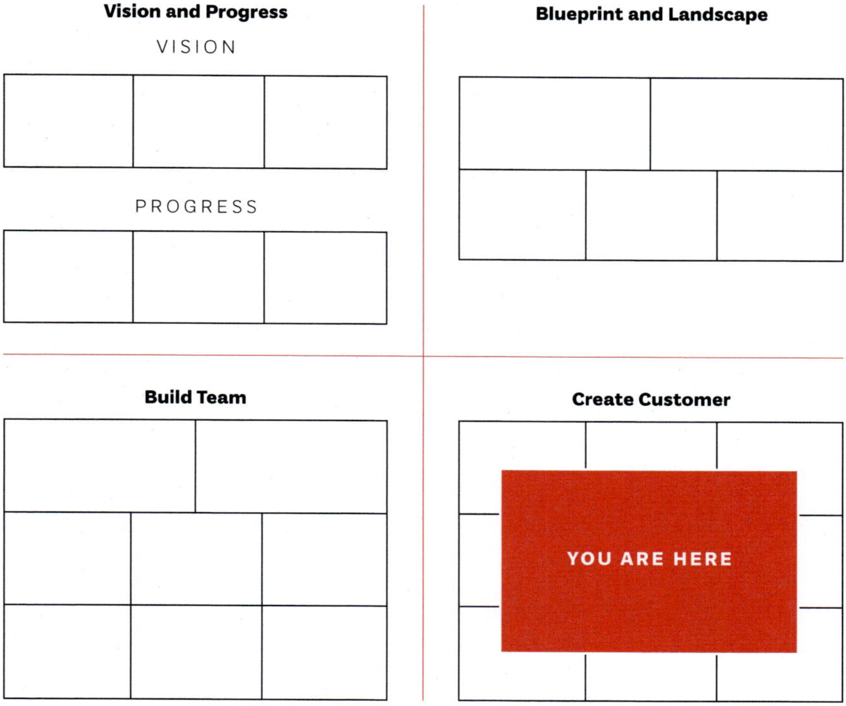

Figure 76 – You are here

You need to know and understand your customers, their needs, and how your solutions meet those needs. That's not enough to survive though: you need to know what markets exist (or identify new markets that could be developed) to sustain your organization, and to identify and understand your opportunities and threats.

When you know this information, you are 'making your own luck' by knowing where the right time and right place is to engage with your customers with the right product/service.

Henry Ford famously said that if he asked what people wanted, they would have asked for faster horses. I have heard this quote used by people who don't want to involve people in designing their products. However, customer insight is the primary information source for product and user experience design.

You may be the product designer yourself, or you may have a team. Your user research needs to be done well if you want to develop a great product, or if you want to know how to turn your product into something great.

Regardless of what they are, your products will be compared by your customers to all of their other relevant experiences. For example, as customers we expect our online shopping experiences to be at least as good as Amazon's in terms of factors such as logistics, ease, returns and refunds. We expect the same level of service in-store. I don't want to feel I need to make a case for something I need to return. We expect government services to be at the same level as private enterprise. We expect our devices and tools to be as intuitive as our smartphones. We increasingly expect our car's features to be upgradeable through the cloud.

These expectations are not only challenges, they are also opportunities.

Apple and Amazon are successful because they know their customers. They provide services and products that their customers find valuable.

Create Customer			
Customer Empathy Map	Value Proposition	Product	**Customer and Product Section**
Geography	Market Segment	Market Comparison	**Market Opportunity Section**
Goals and Metrics	Roadmap	Costs	**Goal Section**

Figure 77 – 'Create Customer' View

REVIEWING YOUR CUSTOMER AND PRODUCT SECTION

You'll recall from Chapter 7 that your customer and product section of your 'Create Customer' view in your visible mission has three sections. We will dig deeper into each section in turn in this chapter.

Customer Empathy

The customer empathy map[64] is a great tool to help you to understand (or develop an understanding of) your customer, and to get to know them as well as they know themselves. Sometimes better than they know themselves.[65]

Some products develop based on 'this is cool: it will be a great product'. These products are usually a solution in search of a problem. Many companies innovate by developing products that they believe the world is dying to have. But they are often wrong, like LG with their InstaView Fridge. I'm sure that some people love the novelty of it. But is it really a product we have been waiting for? Even though you can design and build something, it doesn't mean that it will be a good product. Like the Segway example that I mentioned in the Introduction to this book.

You have to know your customer. You have to know what they are struggling with. You have to know what they are trying to do. You have to know how they are solving their problems today, or if they are even solving their problems at all.

Customer empathy is not about products. It is also not just about knowing your customers. It requires caring about our customers, and making their lives better.

If you want to create customers, then you better understand them. Figure 78 provides a template you can use to create your own customer empathy map.

---

64 The original creation of the customer empathy map is attributed to Dave Gray, www.accenture.com/us-en/blogs/software-engineering-blog/what-is-an-empathy-map.

65 I don't mean that in the Facebook/Cambridge Analytica sense. I mean it in the empathy/caring sense.

Figure 78 – Customer empathy map template

Customer Empathy Workshop

Purpose/Outcome: to develop empathy with your customers.

Suggested duration: half a day.

Frequency: at least as frequent as your goal cycle planning. All participants should keep a copy of your customer empathy map handy. It should be updated as they get to know more about your customers. If the boxes in the template are not appropriate, then change them until they work to help you understand your customers.

Participation: your customer service, product, marketing and sales teams.

Additional Resources: *Value Proposition Design* by Osterwalder, Pigneur, Bernada and Smith[66], *The Outside-in Corporation* by Bund[67], and again, *UX for Lean Startups: Faster, Smarter User Experience Research and Design* by Laura Klein.[68] (Even though the title for the latter includes the words "lean startups", everyone should be using this approach.)

Value Proposition

Many organizations are obsessed about their products. Yet they often struggle to talk about their value propositions.

The value proposition is a description of how your product will relieve your customers of their pain, and/or provide a gain that they might not have asked for, or even thought about. It looks at your product from a customer perspective.

This perspective is critical since it forces you and your team to put yourselves in the shoes of your customers. This is a reality check, especially if you are new to customer-centric design. The value proposition applies whether your customers are individuals, or other businesses or organizations. Figure 79 provides a template you can use to create your value proposition.

---

66 *Value Proposition Design*, Osterwalder, Pigneur, Bernarda and Smith (2014), Wiley.

67 *The Outside-In Corporation*, Bund (2005), McGraw-Hill.

68 *UX for Lean Startups: Faster, Smarter User Experience Research and Design* by Laura Klein (2108), O'Reilly Media.

Value Proposition	
Customer Segment	
Product	
Pain Reliever	
Gain Creator	

Figure 79 – Value proposition template

Value Proposition Workshop

Purpose/Outcome: to accurately describe your value proposition for your customers.

Suggested duration: As long as it takes to confirm what is valuable to your customers.

Frequency: during your goal cycle planning and product development phases.

Participants: your customer service professionals, and your product, marketing and sales teams.

Additional resources: *Value Proposition Design* by Osterwalder, Pigneur, Bernada and Smith[69] is a great general resource.

Product/Service

If you're like most organizations, you will have your products/services and their features well-defined.This information is your product/service detail, description, cost, value, etc.[70] This section of the 'Create Customer' view of your visible mission is also where you can collect additional product/service information: lead time, shelf life, versions, etc.

If your customer segments and markets have been defined, they could be added or linked to each product/service. You can extend your basic data to show the potential value of your products/services in markets where you are not currently engaged. Figure 80 provides a template you can use.

---

69 *Value Proposition Design,* Osterwalder, Pigneur, Bernarda and Smith (2014), Wiley.

70 Where applicable, I recommend including what problem each product/service feature solves for the customer, and how each one contributes to your business goals. This is valuable information to help you understand what product/service features you should be investing in, and which ones you shouldn't. The Lean UX approach is highly recommended.

Product	
Description	
Price	
Target Date	
Cost	
Customer Segment	
Market Size	
Market Share	
Market Value	
Assumptions	

Figure 80 – Product detail template

Product/Service Workshop

Purpose/Outcome: to define your product/service features in terms of the problems they solve for your customers.

Suggested duration: as long as it takes.

Frequency: as often as your goal cycle planning, and during your product design meetings.

Participation: your customer service, product, marketing and sales teams.

Additional resources: *Lean UX* by Gothelf and Seiden[71], and *UX for Lean Startups: Faster, Smarter User Experience Research and Design* by Laura Klein.[72]

REVIEWING YOUR MARKET SECTION

You'll recall from Chapter 7 that your market section of your 'Create Customer' view in your visible mission has three sections. We will now dig deeper into each section.

Geography

Your customer geography is an important aspect of your opportunities and challenges. Even if you intend to have a global market, most organizations usually start off smaller. This helps to clear out any wrinkles in production, marketing and sales channels, including logistics, delivery and support. However, if you are a local business, it might be both useful and interesting to look at other opportunities beyond your city's limits.

I like looking at a map of my customer markets – it gives me a sense of my customers' reality. Who are they, where do they live, and what

---

71 *Lean UX,* Gothelf and Seiden (2016), O'Reilly Media.

72 *UX for Lean Startups: Faster, Smarter User Experience Research and Design* by Laura Klein (2018), O'Reilly Media.

do their lives look like? Refer back to Figure 26 in Chapter 7 as an example of El Jefe's customer geography.

Geography Workshop

Purpose/Outcome: to understand more about your existing and potential geographic markets.

Suggested duration: 1 hour.

Frequency: as often as your goal cycle planning.

Participants: your product, marketing, sales and customer service teams.

TO DO

Capture key information about each geographic location:

- what is the total population?
- what are the characteristics of the people?
- what does the culture look like?
- how accessible is the area?
- why would you be interested in engaging with customers in a new location?
- why would these potential customers be interested in your value proposition?

Market Segment

Market segment value is based on the market size (i.e. the total number of the customers in a market) and the market share that you have (or can capture). The more market share you can capture, the higher your revenue and profit. Make sure the numbers that you base each market segment value on in your visible mission are realistic.

You may also find it useful to note how much competition there is in a particular market, and any challenges or opportunities associated with each one. If you have specific costs associated with particular markets (like shipping, warehousing, etc.), this would be the place to add this information in your visible mission.

It's also useful to plan and estimate a customer acquisition rate. Your forecast lets you create a realistic estimate of market revenue. It's important to understand that it's unlikely that you will be able to hit your intended market share immediately. Estimate a growth trajectory instead. This in turn will enable you to plan the financial aspects to fund your market expansion. Figure 81 shows a growth trajectory for Le Jefe based on their social media activity.

Week	Twitter Followers	Re-tweets	Facebook Likes	Meal / Day	Hours / Day	Week Meals
01.06.14	1500	200	50	20	1	100
08.06.14	1650	240	58	30	1	150
15.06.14	1815	288	66	40	2	200
22.06.14	1997	346	76	50	2	250
29.06.14	2196	415	87	80	3	400
06.07.14	2416	498	101	100	3	500
13.07.14	2657	597	116	120	4	600
20.07.14	2923	717	133	180	5	900
27.07.14	3215	860	153	200	6	1000
03.08.14	3537	1032	176	220	6	1100
10.08.14	3891	1238	202	250	6	1250
17.08.14	4280	1486	233	180	6	1400

Figure 81 – Customer acquisition data, partial list (El Jefe)

Monitoring your customer acquisition rate will help you to track and adjust your activities accordingly. For example, if your new customer acquisition rate is higher than your forecast, you need to be able to ensure that your capabilities keep up with the higher demand. Right-sizing your ability to sell, deliver, distribute, and support your customers is very important.

Figure 82 shows that there is a limit to the amount of meals that can be served per day and per week by chef Carl in his Le Jefe food truck business (the thick yellow and green lines, respectively). If his daily and weekly demand reaches those levels, he can decide if it would be viable to get another food truck.

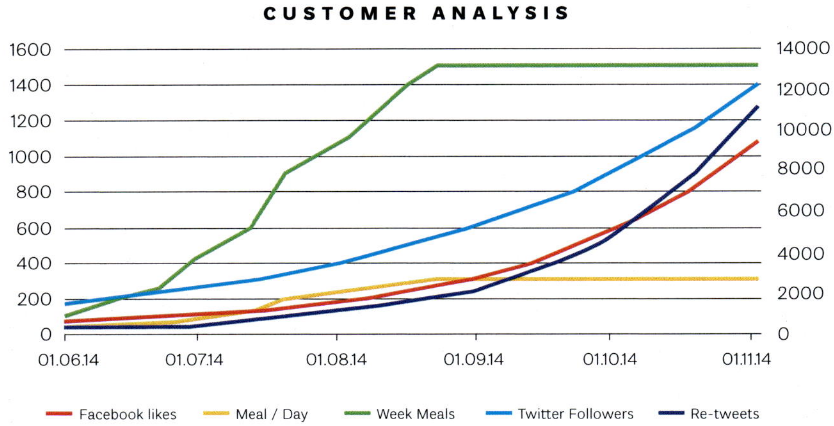

Figure 82 – Customer acquisition metrics (Le Jefe)

Even though you may know certain things (e.g. there is an obvious limit to the number of products you can produce or services you can deliver with your current capacity), seeing that information visually in a graph makes the limit and its implications clearer for everyone. Figure 83 provides a template that you can use.

Segment	
Description	
Product	
Price	
Market Size	
Market Share	
Number of Customers	
Cost	
Cost Notes	
Assumptions	

Figure 83 – Market segment template

Market Segment Workshop

Purpose/Outcome: to determine the value of your current and potential market segments.

Suggested duration: this information should be prepared in advance by your marketing, sales and product teams – based on estimates, research, etc.

Since this information is critical for your goals and building out your vision, you should take the appropriate amount of time to work through it. Of course, the amount of time will depend on what your investment needs to be, the size of the opportunity, etc. The bigger the market segment and any associated risk, the more you need to understand it. You could decide to test the market with either market research, or set up a temporary store in a particular location.

Frequency: as often as your goal cycle planning.

Participants: your marketing, sales, product, logistics and customer service teams.

Market Comparison

The core of strategy is deciding which market segments to engage with. To make that decision, you need to know your options, and be able to compare them. Your options depend on your:

- product,
- channels,
- customer segments,
- value proposition,
- business model, and
- competition.

In some cases, you may stumble into a market, or default to one that seems the most obvious.

However, you should evaluate our chances of success with each option, and then decide whether or not to engage. Even if engaging with a particular market may seem obvious and intuitive, taking a thoughtful and analytical approach can open your eyes to possibilities that you might not have considered before.

For example, a closer look may show that you are about to wade into a market that's red with the 'blood' of the competition. Maybe there is a better option to explore. If you think you don't have any options, then it's very likely that you aren't looking hard enough. Necessity is the mother of invention, including finding market options.

Segment	Location	Population	Market Share	Cost	Custimers	Avg / Cost	Revenue	Porofit	Segment Total
Segment A	Location 1								
	Location 2								
	Location 3								
Segment B	Location 1								
	Location 2								
	Location 3								

Figure 84 – Market comparison template

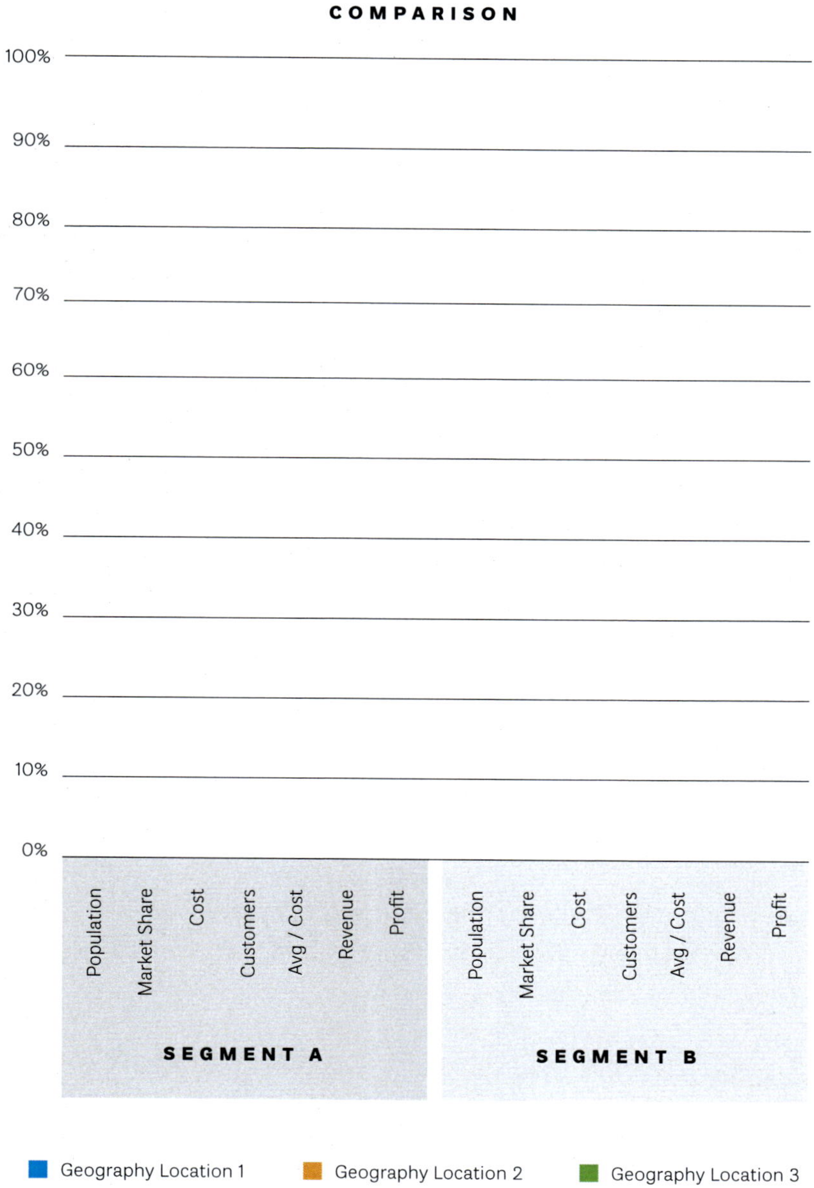

Figure 85 – Market comparison graph template

Market Comparison Workshop

Purpose/Outcome: compare different market options to help you decide which markets to engage with.

Suggested duration: at least half a day. The duration will depend on your:

- business,
- market segment values,
- investment,
- risks, and
- opportunities.

The importance of this workshop makes the time and attention invested in it worth its weight in gold.

Frequency: at least during the preparation and planning for each goal cycle. The market segments that you consider will get additional attention during the establishment of your goals, metrics and initiatives. You can use that information to refine your choices of which markets to engage with – i.e. confirming, changing, postponing your entry or even scrapping your entry into some market segments.

Participants: your leadership team.

REVIEWING YOUR GOALS SECTION

You'll recall from Chapter 7 that your market section of your 'Create Customer' view in your visible mission has three sections. We will now dig deeper into each section.

Goals, Metrics and Initiatives

If market choice is the core of strategy, then goals are the description of strategy's success. Each goal should be made up of a set of metrics – things that are measurable. However, there should not be too many metrics. Three metrics is a good number. If you have too many more, then it becomes more challenging to focus your efforts. They get diffused, and success can slip away.

SMART metrics

Each metric should have SMART characteristics. SMART is an acronym for specific, measurable, assignable, realistic and time-bound.

- **Specific**: the metric addresses a specific area or 'thing', e.g. Twitter followers.
- **Measurable**: the metric can be measured. For example, acquire 100 Twitter followers.
- **Assignable**: somebody is responsible for achieving the metric, and is given access to the necessary resources, or the ability to acquire those resources.
- **Realistic**: It is considered realistic by the planners, the responsible person, and the resources. It is 100 new followers, not a million.
- **Time-bound**: There is a target date associated with the goal. The target date: before the end of the summer.

Let's use chef Carl's El Jefe example again. Figure 86 shows that he has four goals planned: an initial test run in Miami, then operating in New Orleans, Austin, and finally at The Brig in Los Angeles.

For each of these goals there are three metrics: the buying of the food, the development of the menu, and the revenue from cooking. For each of these metrics there is work, effort, expenses, and time associated. Recording this information will help Carl to understand if the revenue he generates will enable him to make a profit.

For example, if his revenue will not cover his basic expenses, or it breaks down to only a small profit in relation to the amount of work and effort involved, then it will reveal that he doesn't have a viable business model. This will force him to figure out what he can do to reduce his costs, increase his revenue, or do both.

Goals	Items	Date		Measure			Effort			Cost		
		Start	Target	Target	Current	Measure Status	Planned	Actual	Effort Status	Planned	Actual	Effort Status
TEST COOKING		06.06.14	06.11.14									
	Buy Food	06.06.14	06.11.14	100	100	100%	4	5	125%	200	300	150%
	Develop Menu	06.06.14	06.11.14	100	100	100%	5	4	80%	20	20	100%
	Cook - Lummus Beach	06.06.14	06.11.14	500	240	48%	16	10	63%	250	300	120%
NEW ORLEANS		06.12.14	06.18.14									
	Buy Food	06.12.14	06.18.14	100	95	95%	4	5	125%	200	230	115%
	Develop Menu	06.12.14	06.18.14	100	100	100%	5	5	100%	20	20	100%
	Cook - Cafe du Monde	06.12.14	06.18.14	1000	1200	120%	16	12	75%	400	420	105%
AUSTIN		06.20.14	06.23.14									
	Buy Food	06.20.14	06.23.14	100	0	0%	4	0	0&	200	0	0%
	Develop Menu	06.20.14	06.23.14	100	0	0%	5	0	0%	20	0	0%
	Cook - Franklin Barbeque	06.20.14	06.23.14	2000	0	0%	16	0	0%	500	0	0%
LOS ANGELES		06.25.14	06.30.14									
	Buy Food	06.25.14	06.30.14	100	0	0%	4	0	0%	200	0	0%
	Develop Menu	06.25.14	06.30.14	100	0	0%	5	0	0%	20	0	0%
	Cook - The Brig	06.25.14	06.30.14	3000	0	0%	16	0	0%	500	0	0%

Figure 86 – Goals and metrics data (El Jefe)

Goals, Metrics and Initiatives Workshop

Purpose/Outcome: to select and refine your best goals, metrics and initiatives. It is important to use your past goal information to ensure your estimates are realistic.

Suggested duration: one week.

Participation: your leadership team.

Frequency: during your goal cycle planning.

Additional resources: *Measure What Matters* by Doerr.[73]

Roadmap

Once your goals and the target dates have been set, they can be shared with the teams who will be working to achieve them. Each team is responsible for creating the plan for their part in achieving the goal. These plans often consist of one or more initiatives per metric,

73 *Measure What Matters*, Doerr (2018), Portfolio.

and each initiative typically has multiple tasks. These initiatives are brought together and coordinated by bringing the teams together and looking at assumptions, interdependencies, resources, etc.

Trust your teams to come up with their plans, but feel free to ask for explanations. After all, you don't want a plan that is unrealistic. It should be based on the team's experience and the resources it has available. Trusting your teams to create plans creates co-ownership of the work, the outcomes they are responsible for, and the results they achieve.

We all work better when we have put our name on something!

Having goals with supporting metrics helps you to focus the attention of everyone in an organization. For example, if new work is pushed in from the side that isn't on the plan, then the team can legitimately ask which goals and metrics are allowed to slip if their efforts are to be applied elsewhere.

Goals	Metrics	Date		Plan Duration	1.6	2.6	3.6	4.6	5.6	6.6	7.6	8.6	9.6	10.6	11.6	12.6	13.6	14.6	15.6	16.6
		Start	Target																	
TEST COOKING		06.06.14	11.06.14																	
	Buy Food	06.06.14	11.06.14	6																
	Develop Menu	06.06.14	11.06.14	6																
	Cook - Lummus Beach	06.06.14	11.06.14	6																
NEW ORLEANS		13.06.14	18.06.14																	
	Buy Food	13.06.14	18.06.14	7																
	Develop Menu	13.06.14	18.06.14	7																
	Cook - Cafe du Monde	13.06.14	18.06.14	7																

Figure 87 – 'Create Customer' roadmap for El Jefe

Roadmap Workshop

Purpose/Outcome: to provide a roadmap for the goal and initiative responsibilities for each team in your organization that you and your leadership team can then coordinate.

Suggested duration: depending on the complexity – one to three days.

Frequency: as often as your goal cycle planning.

Participants: teams responsible for achieving your goals, including project managers, partners and agencies. Their initiatives are then coordinated by you and your leadership team.

Costs

Each planned initiative in your roadmap should have a realistic cost forecast associated with it in terms of people, tools, technologies, travel, etc. This amount should then be compared to the actual cost of the initiative when it is implemented, as shown in the Figure 88 and 89 examples. Your forecast costs can also be compared to your forecast revenue for the goal cycle to help you plan your finances.

Goals	Metrics	Cost		
		Planned	Actual	Cost Status
TEST COOKING				
	Buy Food	200	300	150%
	Develop Menu	20	20	100%
	Cook - Lummus Beach	250	300	120%
NEW ORLEANS				
	Buy Food	200	230	115%
	Develop Menu	20	20	100%
	Cook - Cafe du Monde	400	420	105%
AUSTIN				
	Buy Food	200	0	0%
	Develop Menu	20	0	0%
	Cook - Franklin Barbeque	500	0	0%
LOS ANGELES				
	Buy Food	200	0	0%
	Develop Menu	20	0	0%
	Cook - The Brig	500	0	0%

Figure 88 – Initiative cost data (El Jefe)

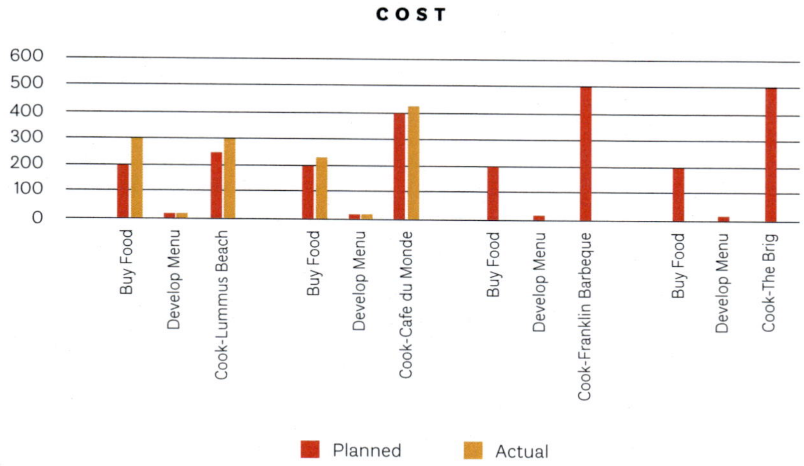

Figure 89 – Graphing initiative costs (El Jefe)

Cost planning and monitoring enables you to re-evaluate your goal choices. You can either confirm your choices, or decide to adjust them. For example, if your first choice is more expensive than you thought, you can go with another goal instead. Or you can lay the groundwork for achieving another goal before getting back to your first choice. Some of its costs may be offset by getting some other basics in place.

Costs Workshop

Purpose/Outcome: to compare the forecast and actual costs of your initiatives.

Suggested duration: half a day to review your plans, and decide whether to proceed, change, or drop a particular goal.

Frequency: as often as your goal cycle planning.

Participants: your leadership team.

Knowing, understanding, and empathizing with your customers is the only way you can reliably create valuable solutions (products or services).

You also need an accessible market of sufficient size and value to make a profit. You need to examine your markets to decide which are the best to engage with, and then set your goals.

Your goals then need to be converted into initiatives and roadmaps with their associated costs forecast and monitored. Doing this will help you to make the best market choices.

Carefully analyzed and selected goals and initiatives allowed NASA to realize their Moon landing vision. They analyzed the critical aspects that had to be addressed, including what was known, and what needed to be known. They were very careful in picking the right technological and managerial 'battles' to fight.

Each of their Apollo space program missions had a number of initiatives with clear outcomes specified. NASA's resources for each effort were planned and coordinated before they became the agreed goals for their missions.

Depending on your situation, you need to select goals to engage with your customers, or to lay the foundation to get to your customers. If you are not generating revenue or making a profit, then the visible mission roadmap will set you on the right path.

But as an organization, what capabilities do you need to achieve the goals for your current cycle? What capabilities do you have to develop to achieve your current goals? These questions will be answered in Chapter 16.

CHAPTER 16

Digging Deeper into Building Your Team

For the Moon landing to become a reality (in fact, for any of its activities), NASA had to develop its organization. An organization is made up of people, sure. But it also includes processes, information, tools and technologies needed to turn its vision into reality.

In order to launch its rockets, NASA needed a launch pad. Its launch pad needed to be built, but that could only be done after it was designed by a team of engineers, architects, designers and builders who had the right equipment, information, and level of experience to make it happen.

This design and building process needed to happen with all of the components of each of NASA's Apollo space program missions – the rocket, the spacecraft, the factories where they were built, etc. Logistics and transportation aspects also had to be considered every step of the way.

Before you can take off with your 'spacecraft' in your visible mission for your organization (and before you can land), you need a runway. But how do you know what kind of runway to build? This chapter will walk you through the process to help you figure out when to build the runway you need, but no more than you need.

To create and keep customers, you need to develop and deliver valuable solutions.

To create valuable solutions, you need the right organization and the right processes (or value streams).

Value streams work by applying people, processes, information, tools and technologies. A collection of people, process, information, tools and technology is called a capability.

It's crucial to evaluate how business-ready your value streams are to achieve your goals. This evaluation should guide your team-building efforts: the people, processes, information, tools and technologies necessary to succeed in the current goal cycle, as well as those that will build the foundation for your next goal cycle.

This cycle-by-cycle approach prevents the overdevelopment of unimportant value streams. It keeps the focus on the key task at hand, while also keeping an eye on the key ones in the near future.

I know that the material in this chapter (and the work that it entails) may at times feel overwhelming. Relax! I will provide a short-cut as well towards the end of the chapter. But it's important to understand the details first. The time and energy that you invest will be worth it in terms of the value it creates.

And the more you go through this team-building process, the faster you will get at it. You will consistently build your organization to achieve what you are planning, goal cycle after goal cycle. It is a rational approach. You will see what capabilities you need to develop, clearly linked to where you need them most.

This cycle-by-cycle approach is a solid way to future-proof the way your organization develops, runs, and continuously improves. It will eliminate the need for quick, symptomatic fixes that both become extremely expensive over time, and so intertwined that they are almost impossible to fix.[74]

Your organization and its ability to learn, adjust, grow and adapt will improve over time when you build the right team to help achieve the amazing things that you imagine.

You are here.

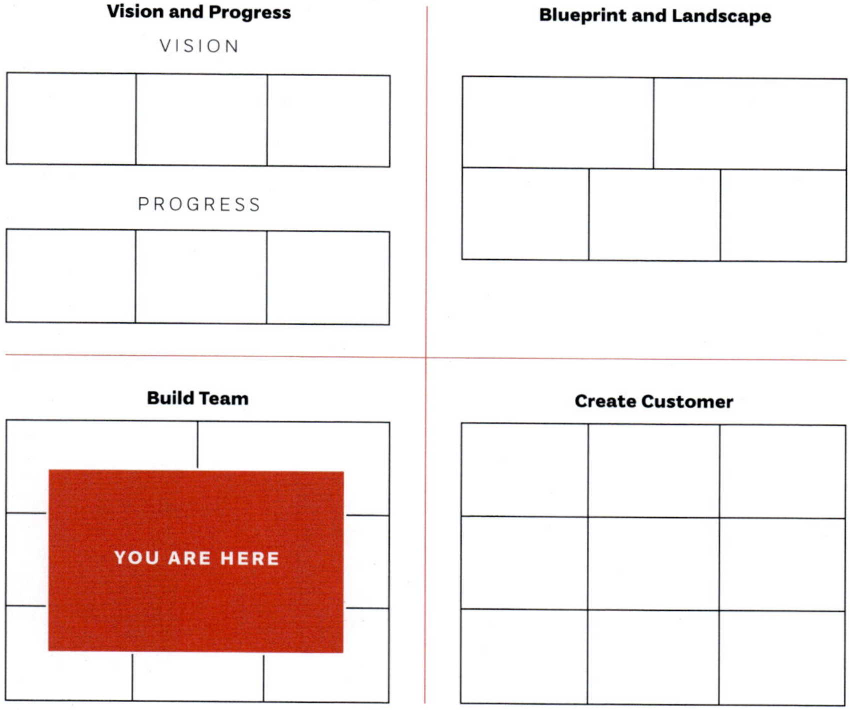

Figure 90 – You are here

We looked at value streams and the elements needed to deliver customer value in Chapter 8. Recall that customers can be external (e.g. our paying customers), or internal (e.g. colleagues and collab-

74 These fixes are typically referred to as 'legacy' solutions (aka 'the really stupid things we did in the past that are now impossible to fix'.

orators, partners, etc.). Also recall that the ‘Build Team’ view of your visible mission (and its associated work) is broken into three sections:

1) value stream (where your team value streams and capabilities are defined),

2) assessment (where your value streams are analyzed and prioritized so that your team improvement needs can be identified), and

3) goals (where your team improvement and strengthening efforts are planned).

Once your ‘Build Team’ goals are planned, they need to be coordinated with your ‘Create Customer’ plans. In some cases, your ‘Create Customer’ plans may have to be adjusted. For example, if your value streams or capabilities can’t be brought to the required maturity level in your current goal cycle, then your ‘Create Customer’ goals may have to be delayed.

You may wonder why we didn’t check your team’s capabilities before planning your ‘Create Customer goals. That would be similar to President Kennedy saying back in the early 1960s, “Let’s shoot a rocket in the sky. We know we can do that.”

Like NASA, you will likely have bigger dreams than you are capable of achieving right now. That’s why planning how to build and strengthen your team is so important.

Build Team			
Capabilties (Key Resources)		Value Streams (Key Activities)	**Value Stream Section**
Value Stream Analysis	Assessment Matrix	Urgency	**Assessment Section**
Goals and Metrics	Roadmap	Costs	**Goal Section**

Figure 91 – ‘Build Team’ view

REVIEWING YOUR VALUE STREAM SECTION

To help you contextualize your value streams and capabilities, here is another look at the Business Model Canvas template from Chapter 14. Your value streams are your key activities and your capabilities are your key resources. These elements of your organization are related.

Figure 92 – Value streams (key activities) and capabilities (key resources) in the Business Model Canvas template

Value Streams (Key Activities)

Chapter 8 outlined that a value stream is a sequence of activities your organization undertakes to deliver on a customer request. Or put slightly differently, value streams deliver something of *value* to a person or a group, either externally (e.g. customer, partner) or internally (e.g. hiring departments, manufacturing, etc.). You have value streams at your organization, whether you call them by that name or not.

The key activities in a single value stream depend not only on capabilities, but also the success of preceding activities. For example, the meal-to-customer value stream in chef Carl's El Jefe business can be broken into a series of key activities:

- customer greeting and requesting order,
- taking and confirming order,
- cooking the order,
- confirming the order and packing,
- receiving payment, and
- handing over the order.

Different activities also require different capabilities such as customer service, cooking, quality assurance, and money management.

You can use the Figure 93 template to list your value streams, the person or team responsible, and the customer deliverable.

YOUR BUSINESS		
Value Streams	**Responsible**	**Deliverable**

Figure 93 – Value stream template (key activities)

If you don't manage any value streams yet, I recommend that you start by defining what you have. Then prioritize what you don't have, and figure out what you need.

How do you know where you need a value stream? Your customers complain. One of the most telling signs that you have an ill-defined value stream[75] is a customer experience that isn't seamlessly integrated.

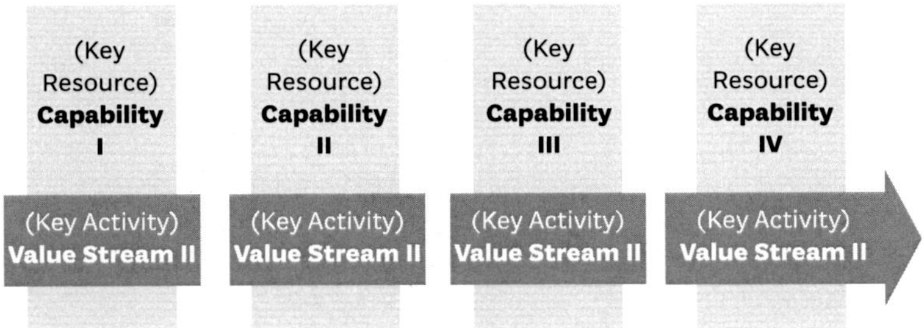

Figure 94 – Fragmented value streams create terrible customer experiences

I have seen the type of fragmentation illustrated in Figure 94 at each large organization where I have worked, especially with multiple customer management and product management systems. Having multiple, fragmented systems is not only financially expensive (as every system is expensive to buy, build or rent, install and maintain, but the real cost is the. organization fragility that comes with technology sprawl.

Let me give you a customer perspective on fragmentation. As a customer of company A, its sales department has a system containing my key data. The marketing department also has a record in their system, because I signed up for a newsletter. The customer support department also has a record, because I called them with a question. None of the systems integrated with the others. I received marketing material for a product where I am already a subscribed customer.

75 If you are interested, Hammer and Champy's *Reengineering the Corporation* is still one of the best books about this problem (and opportunity).

To make matters worse, company A merged with company B (and I am a customer of company B's as, and they have 5 different systems where they carry my data). Since this is now one company, I expect to be able to change my contact details once, and that will be the end of it. However, I would be wrong, because none of their systems are integrated.

In many organizations, this fragmentation happens because each department tends to develop its own capabilities (e.g. customer relationship management). When developing their systems, they often don't think about collaborating with other departments that already have the same (or similar) systems and capabilities. Or they may try, but then they feel that an integrated system will slow their work down because decisions about its joint capabilities need to be shared.

This is made worse when the performance metrics in organizations are focused on departments, rather than performance metrics for collaboration. If departments have their own budgets for capabilities, then this contributes to the fragmentation of capabilities (especially technology sprawl).

However, it's also important to note that in some cases it does make sense to have the same capability implemented and managed individually in different organizational departments. For example, if your organization employs people globally, then you may need a HR system for each country that reflects local laws and market conditions. The same may be true for your accounting system (although some tax management systems have multinational capabilities). The bottom line is that to standardize where it will undermine your ability to function makes little sense: you need to find the best approach between integration and non-integration depending on each specific circumstance. Your decision should depend on your business goals and needs.

Value Stream Workshop

Purpose/Outcome: to review (or define) your value streams.

Suggested duration: 1 hour.

Frequency: as often as your goal cycle planning, unless you are making strategic changes to organization.

Participants: your leadership team and process leads.

Additional resources: *Value Stream Mapping* by Martin and Osterling.[76] See also *Mapping Experiences*: *A Guide to Creating Value Through Journeys, Blueprints, and Diagrams* by Kalbach[77] (O'Reilly, 2016).

Capabilities (Key Resources)

You can think of your key resources (capabilities) as being tools in your toolbox (i.e. they are static). However, your tools will realize their full value when you apply them in your key activities (value streams) (i.e. they will become dynamic).

As outlined in Chapter 8, your key resources are often shown and thought of individually, but they should be packaged as part of a capability. Your people, processes, information, tools and technologies are all resources, but they function as a capability. Capabilities are important business execution skills. They are typically grouped by focus area (e.g. customer service, HR, product management, accounting, etc.). These focus areas tend to have specific processes and information that both need to be managed. For example, chef Carl uses an app to manage the accounting function in his El Jefe business. It has processes that enable customers to pay him and for the information associated with the transaction to be recorded so that reports can be produced.

Figure 95 provides a template you can use to list your capabilities, the person or team responsible, any relevant comments, and the cost.

---

76 *Value Stream Mapping,* Martin and Osterling, McGraw Hill, 2013.

77 *Mapping Experiences,* Kalbach, O'Reilly Media, 2021.

Capabilities (Key Resource / Function)	Responsible	Comments	Cost

Figure 95 – Capability list template

Capabilities Workshop

Purpose/Outcome: to review (or define) your organization's capabilities (key resources)

Suggested duration: 1 hour.

Frequency: as often as your goal cycle planning, or if you are making strategic changes to your organization.

Participants: your leadership team and functional leads.

REVIEWING YOUR ASSESSMENT SECTION

Now that you have your value streams and capabilities reviewed or defined, you can check how well they are functioning to meet the demands of your 'Create Customer' goals. Recall from Chapter 8 that your assessment section of your visible mission contains three sections:

1) value stream analysis,

2) assessment matrix, and

3) urgency.

We will now dig deeper into each one in turn. There is also an abbreviated assessment section at the end of the chapter. It provides a quick, narrow assessment, however using it misses out on getting buy-in from your teams.

Value Stream Analysis

Value stream analysis involves gathering information to determine the priority, the current, state, and the future need for each value stream. After the information is gathered, you will be able to produce an assessment matrix to show where you and your team are today, where you want to be, and the urgency graph – which shows you the relative urgency of the value stream work that needs to be done to help you achieve your 'Create Customer' goals. Figure 96 provides a useful value stream analysis template that you can use.

Value Stream	
Description	
Deliverable	
Priority	
Current Readiness	
Future Readiness	
Integration	
Standardization	
Cost	
Cost Notes	
Assumptions	
Recommendation	

Figure 96 – Value stream analysis template

Prioritization

Start by taking an objective approach to prioritizing your value streams. (In organizations where an objective approach isn't used, the person with the most influence, the loudest voice, or sometimes the most annoying person will often prevail, even when the development of another value stream is more important.)

So, how do you objectively prioritize your value streams? You cross-reference your 'Create Customer' goals with your value streams.

I recommend that each member of your leadership team writes a short rationale for each value stream's relative importance. You and your team might have an instinctive rating, but when you are forced to provide your rationale (even to yourselves), it will help to make your rating more rational and accurate.[78] These rationales also facilitate the discussion of significant outliers – participants can share their rationales. One may have a valuable insight that others have overlooked.

It's also common for people to use perceived gaps and weaknesses as a way to prioritize. There is no place for this when using the visible mission approach. Your value stream's priority is based on its contribution to your 'Create Customer' goals.

Participants can use their rationale to assign a 5-point rating to a value stream's importance:

- a 5 can be assigned when a value stream is critical for the execution of a 'Create Customer' goal.
- a 3 can be assigned when it is playing a supporting role.
- a 1, 2 or 4 can be assigned where appropriate.

If the value stream has no bearing whatsoever on your 'Create Customer' goal, then can be left blank. At the end, the total score for each capability is its relative importance in terms of its impact on your 'Create Customer' goals. The higher the score, the higher the priority.

78 Thank Daniel Kahneman's Thinking Fast and Slow for this approach.

Figure 97 provides an example of value stream prioritization for Le Jefe.

EL JEFE	Priority (5 point rating)					
Value Streams	**Total**	**Truck**	**Miami**	**New Orleans**	**Austin**	**Los Angeles**
Options-to-Events	**14**	0	2	3	4	5
Shopping-to-Ingredients	**13**	0	1	2	5	5
Ingredient-to-Menu	**12**	0	1	2	4	5
Event-to-Awareness	**14**	0	2	3	4	5
Event-to-Permit	**20**	0	5	5	5	5
Work-to-Pay	**15**	3	3	3	3	3
Budget-to-Actual	**9**	1	2	2	2	2
Customer-to-Meal	**23**	3	5	5	5	5
Health-Ready (cleaning)	**25**	5	5	5	5	5
Bill-to-Paid	**8**	0	2	2	2	2
Use-to-Run (maint.)	**13**	5	2	2	2	2

Figure 97 – Value stream prioritization (Le Jefe)

Value Stream Analysis Workshop (Part 1 – Prioritization)

Purpose/Outcome: to prioritize the importance of each of your value streams.

Suggested duration: 1 hour.

Frequency: as often as your goal cycle planning, unless your goals change before the end of your cycle.

Participants: your leadership team. (If you have an enterprise architect, I recommend including her/him as an observer for the context provided by the leadership team.)

Current State and Future Needs

After you have prioritized your value streams, you can move onto the next stage: establishing the current state of your value streams and capabilities.

Part 1 of your value stream analysis workshop outlined earlier used your leadership team to prioritize your value streams. Analyzing the current state of your value streams and capabilities should be done separately to get better results. If the two analyses are conflated, the biggest perceived value stream gaps inevitably get all the attention.

Instead of using your leadership team to assess the current state of your value streams and capabilities, use your frontline workers, team leads, and managers responsible for each value stream.

The current state rating is done for each value stream and is based on four aspects:

1) people,

2) process,

3) information, and

4) tools and technologies.

It's important to look at all four aspects because if any are addressed in isolation, you may end up solving the wrong problem. For example, spending a lot of money on a new system without addressing your business processes is not going to solve your problems – it might make them worse.

Your participants should provide a numerical rating for the current state of each value stream on each of the four aspects, using the five-point scale:

- a 5 can be assigned where the value stream is self-improving.
- a 3 can be assigned where the value stream is OK – not terrible, but not great either.
- a 0 can indicate that the value stream has not been defined as such, or is not currently being managed.
- 1, 2 and 4 can be used as appropriate.

As with your prioritization, each person in your workshop to analyze your current state should write a short rationale for their rating of each aspect for each value stream. The rationale helps to ground each rating, and facilitates discussion. It's not uncommon for one person in an organization to be aware of a weakness in a value stream or capability that others may not be.

After the current state is determined, your participants should indicate the level that each aspect of the value stream (i.e. people, process, information, and tools and technologies) should be at to achieve its 'Create Customer' goal. Your participants should also describe what should be done to reach the required level. By encouraging this information, you are laying the foundations for the improvement goals, metrics and initiatives that you will then define to strengthen your value streams.

Figure 98 provides an example of the current state of each of Le Jefe's value streams.

EL JEFE		Current State (5 point rating)					Future Need (5 point rating)				
Value Streams	Respons.	Total	People	Process	Tools	Info	Total	People	Process	Tools	Info
Options-to-Events	Carl	11	3	3	2	3	14	3	3	4	4
Shopping-to-Ingredients	Carl	8	2	2	2	2	12	4	3	2	3
Ingredient-to-Menu	Carl	17	4	4	4	5	18	5	4	4	5
Event-to-Awareness	Tony	8	2	2	2	2	12	3	3	3	3
Event-to-Permit	Carl	10	3	2	3	2	15	4	3	5	3
Work-to-Pay	Carl	20	5	5	5	5	20	5	5	5	5
Budget-to-Actual	Tony	15	3	3	4	5	15	3	3	4	5
Customer-to-Meal	Carl	18	5	4	4	5	19	5	5	4	5
Health-Ready (cleaning)	Tony	16	5	3	3	5	18	5	4	4	5
Bill-to-Paid	Carl	12	3	3	3	3	12	3	3	3	3
Use-to-Run (maint.)	Tony	7	2	2	2	1	9	3	2	2	2

Figure 98 – Current states and future needs of value streams (El Jefe)

Value Stream Analysis Workshop (Part 2 – Current State and Future Needs)

Purpose/Outcome: to analyze the current state and future needs assessments for each of your value streams.

Suggested duration: workshop preparation – 8 hours, workshop – 2 hours.

Frequency: as often as your goal cycle planning.

Participants: your frontline workers, managers, and enterprise architect (if you have one); your leadership team as observers. (It is important to include representatives from your front-line workers, since they are most likely to be able to tell you what is missing, and what is needed.)

Assessment Matrix

Your assessment matrix will provide you with an easy-to-read visualization of the state of your value streams. Create it as a scatter chart with two axes. Label the horizontal axis 'Priority' and the vertical axis 'Current State', as illustrated in the Figure 99 template.

The priority of your value streams will be based on the ratings in your Value Stream Analysis Part 1 Workshop.

The current state of your value streams will be based on the ratings in your Value Stream Analysis Part 2 Workshop.

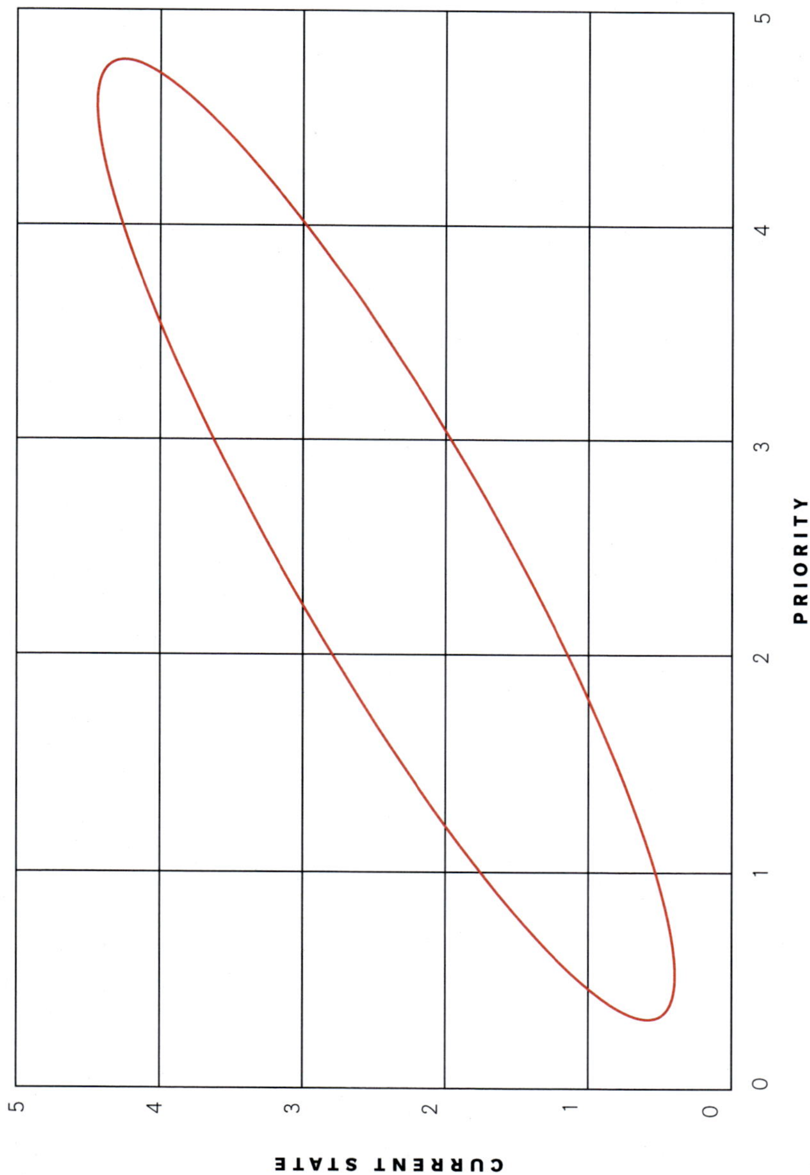

Figure 99 – Template: current value stream assessment matrix

The priority of each of your value streams will be reflected on the horizontal axis – the further to the right it is, the more important it is.

The current state will be shown on the vertical axis – the higher it is, the better.

As outlined in Chapter 8, the way to read this assessment matrix is to imagine a sweet spot running from the lower left to the upper right. This is where your value streams should lie. The more important a value stream is, the higher your current state for it should be (and vice versa).

You can also create an assessment matrix for the future needs of your value streams. Once again, the priority of your value streams (the horizontal axis) will be based on the ratings in your Value Stream Analysis Part 1 Workshop. The future needs of your value streams (the vertical axis) will be based on the ratings in your Value Stream Analysis Part 2 Workshop. Figure 100 provides a template that you can use.

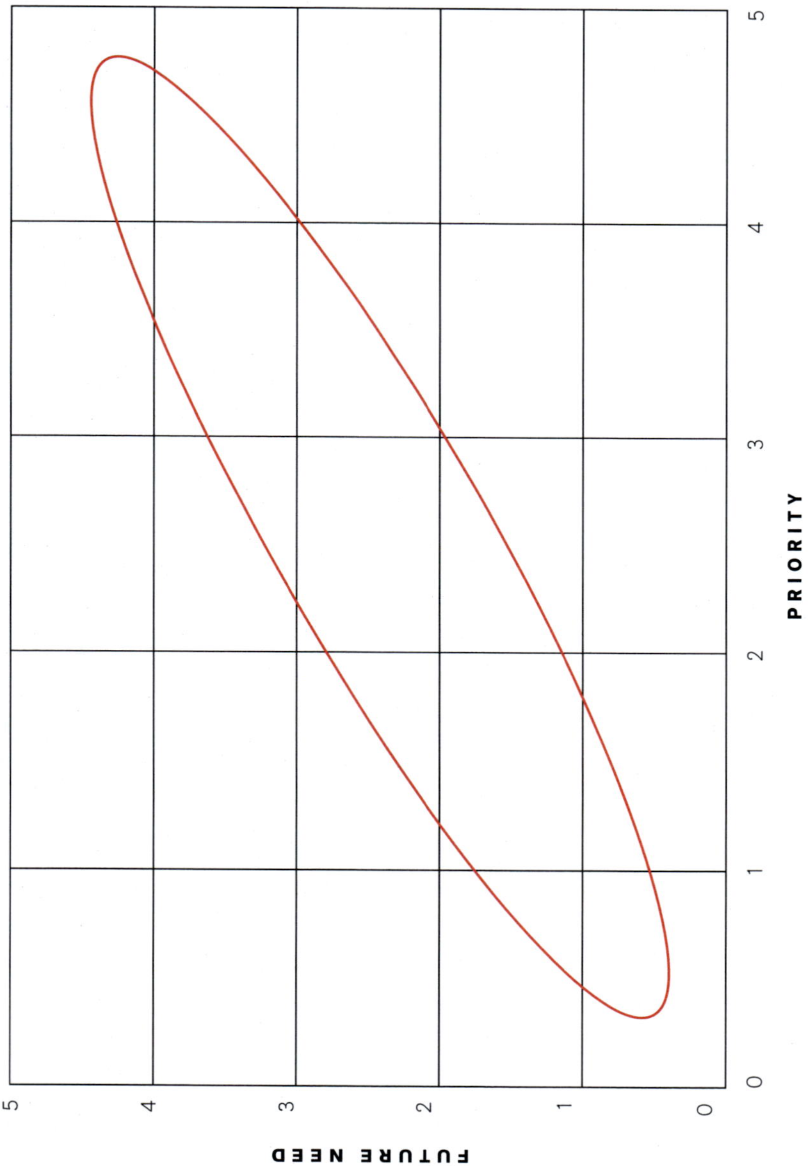

Figure 100 – Template: future value stream assessment matrix. Satisfying your future needs should move each of your capabilities closer to the sweet spot.

Assessment Matrix Workshop

Purpose/Outcome: general guidance and decisions about which value stream issues are to be addressed (first) and what should be done.

Suggested duration: 1 hour (depending on the complexity of your value streams and problems identified, as well as their interdependencies.) The point is not to necessarily solve all your value stream and capability problems in the current goal cycle, but to help prioritize which problems should be addressed first.

Frequency: as often as your goal cycle planning.

Participants: your leadership team and enterprise architect (if you have one).

Standardization and Integration Assessment

The standardization and integration assessment[79] is an additional evaluation option to consider, depending on your knowledge of the fragmentation of your environments. This assessment allows your participants to rate a particular capability in terms of its current state of *standardization* (rating it 5 when one system is used throughout your organization, and 1 when every instance has its own system. (The example of the multiple systems for my customer data that I shared earlier in the chapter would clearly qualify as a 1!)).

In addition, you can use it to assess your current level of *integration* across multiple value streams by using the same approach – 5 when a capability is well integrated (e.g. with API, web services, etc.), and a 0 when a capability is a standalone, inaccessible system that isn't integrated where it should be.

For both analyses, the ideal state of standardization and integration should be stated, and accompanied by rationales.

---

79 *Based on Enterprise Architecture as Strategy,* Ross, Weill and Robertson, 2006 (Harvard Business Review Press).

Urgency

The urgency graph is another easy-to-read visualization tool. It can be used along with your value stream matrices to help you decide which value stream issues (i.e. gaps) to address first.

The urgency of a value stream issue is calculated by multiplying the gap (between its current state and its future need) by the value stream's priority score. The bigger the gap and the higher the priority, the higher the urgency score will be.

Figure 101 shows the urgency data for each of El Jefe's value streams. It reveals that the 'Event-to-Permit' value stream is the most urgent. The gap between its current state and El Jefe's future need is 5 (i.e. 15 minus 10), and its future need score is 20, resulting in an urgency score of 100 (i.e. 5 x 20). This urgency score is significantly higher than the scores for any of his other value streams. Without permits, Carl cannot do anything. He needs to solve this value stream issue – fast!

EL JEFE	**Current State**	**Future Need**			**Priority**
Value Streams	**Total**	**Total**	**Gap**	**Urgency**	**Total**
Options-to-Events	**11**	**14**	3	42	**14**
Shopping-to-Ingredients	**8**	**12**	4	52	**13**
Ingredient-to-Menu	**17**	**18**	1	12	**12**
Event-to-Awareness	**8**	**12**	4	56	**14**
Event-to-Permit	**10**	**15**	5	100	**20**
Work-to-Pay	**20**	**20**	0	0	**15**
Budget-to-Actual	**15**	**15**	0	0	**9**
Customer-to-Meal	**18**	**19**	1	23	**23**
Health-Ready (cleaning)	**16**	**18**	2	50	**25**
Bill-to-Paid	**12**	**12**	0	0	**8**
Use-to-Run (maint.)	**7**	**9**	2	26	**13**

Figure 101 – Urgency data (El Jefe)

Figure 102 is a graph of El Jefe's urgency data which highlights the relative urgency of each value stream.

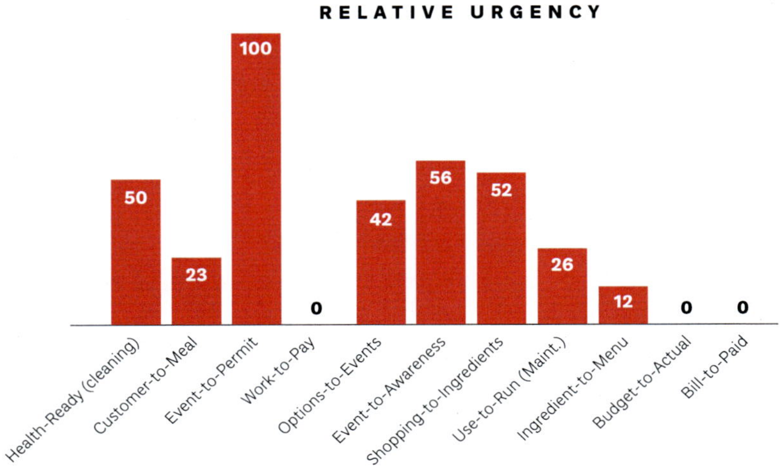

Figure 102 – Relative urgency graph (El Jefe)

Urgency Workshop

Purpose/Outcome: to help you decide which value stream issues (i.e. gaps) to address first.

Suggested duration: 1 hour. The graph can be easily produced when the data is compiled in a spreadsheet.

Frequency: as often as your goal cycle planning.

Participants: your leadership team

REVIEWING YOUR GOALS SECTION

Recall from Chapter 8 that your goals section of your visible mission contains three sections:

1) goals and metrics,

2) roadmap, and

3) costs.

We will now dig deeper into each one in turn.

Goals and Metrics

At this point, you should have the following sets of information for your visible mission:

- your 'Create Customer' goals, metrics, and initiatives,
- your value stream matrices,
- your urgency graph, and
- details of what issues need to be fixed for each value stream.

Your 'Build Team' goals and metrics will focus on closing your value stream gaps based on their relative urgency. Closing these gaps will help you to achieve your 'Create Customer' goals and metrics.

For example, Figures 101 and 102 earlier in the chapter revealed that chef Carl's highest priority is closing the gap for his Event-to-Permit value stream. He therefore needs to create a related 'Build Team' goal and metric for this value stream. This goal should also be placed in the context of his 'Create Customer' goals – participating in events, and selling great food to the customers.

Understanding the context of your 'Create Customer' intent is important for the team responsible for fixing your value stream issues to understand. The value stream improvement work is sometimes added as a metric in the related 'Create Customer' goal. It is up to you and your team to decide what makes the most sense.

However, if your 'Build Team' value stream goals and metrics are defined outside of your 'Create Customer' goals and metrics, they should still be coordinated with those goals. Some of your 'Create Customer' work may be dependent on your 'Build Team' value stream work. Your 'Create Customer' initiatives and roadmaps should be adjusted as needed. (Always remember that your 'runway' needs to be built before your 'plane' can take off or land.)

Figure 103 provides you with a template you can use for your 'Build Team' value stream goals and metrics.

Goals	Metrics	Date			Measure			Effort			Cost		
		Start	Target	Plan Duration	Target	Current	Measure Goal	Planned	Actual	Effort Goal	Planned	Actual	Cost Goal

Figure 103 – 'Build Team' goals and metrics template

Goals and Metrics Workshop

Purpose/Outcome: to outline your 'Build Team' value stream goals, metrics and initiatives.

Suggested duration: 1 hour.

Frequency: as often as your goal cycle planning.

Participants: your leadership team, value stream team, and enterprise architect (if you have one).

Once you define your goals and metrics, they should be assigned to the team responsible for developing your value stream solutions. The team should be given time to consider and confirm the goal intent and its metrics. Once this is done, they should define initiatives related to the goals and metrics, along with an estimate of dates, effort required and likely costs.

Roadmap

Your 'Build Team' roadmap is a date-based visualization of the initiatives that will be executed to achieve your value stream goals. This roadmap is very useful during the discussion of dependencies between different initiatives. For example, if you have the need for a customer support team (a 'Build Team' initiative) to be in place, trained, and having access to the appropriate equipment before your new app is rolled out (a 'Create Customer' initiative).

Figure 104 provides a template you can use for your 'Build Team' roadmap. Roadmaps are usually produced by project or scrum management systems. Use whatever software you have, but find a way to show all the relevant efforts.

Goals	Items	Dates			Calendar											
		Start	Target	Duration												

Figure 104 – 'Build Team' roadmap template

Roadmap Workshop

Purpose/Outcome: to provide a date-based visualization of the initiatives that will be executed to achieve your value stream goals.

Suggested duration: 1 hour, depending on the complexity of the work.

Frequency: as often as your goal cycle planning.

Participants: your leadership and team leads.

Cost

Your cost chart in your visible mission is a representation of the cost per goal, metric and initiative. Each of your initiatives should contain all relevant costs – work, resources, other expenses, etc.

You need all your costs itemized to help you make decisions based on their financial implications (such as scaling back an initiative, or securing funding to pay for it). This information will also be used to eventually track your actual expenses against your planned expenses.

You need to make sure that your investments in strengthening your value streams will pay off. This is difficult to do when analyzing purely in terms of costs, but it's an important decision consideration, along with the priority of a value stream and your related capabilities. If you base a 'Build Team' decision exclusively on cost, then the necessary work is more likely to be delayed. If it is, this will cost you more in the long run, especially if you won't be able to run your business. For example, although there is no direct income for chef Carl from an initiative like truck maintenance, if he neglects to spend money ensuring his truck will run, it might break down or even cause an accident.

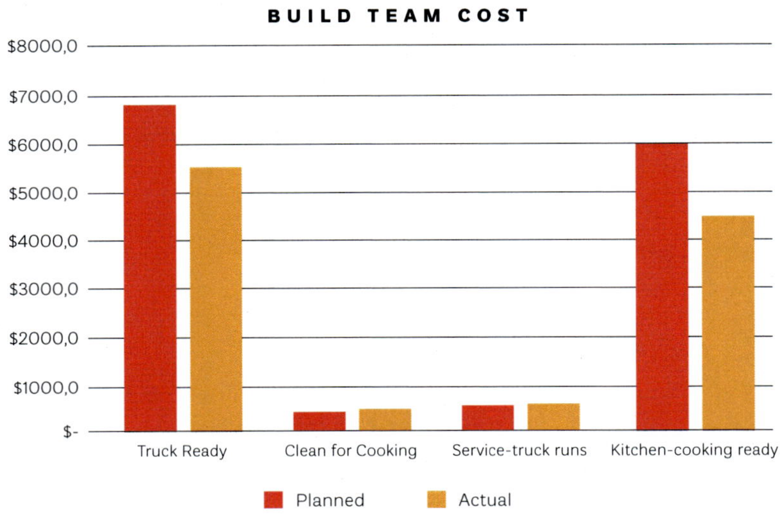

Figure 105 – 'Build Team' planned versus actual cost chart (El Jefe)

Cost Workshop

Purpose/Outcome: to forecast the costs of your 'Build Team' goals, metrics and initiatives to help you make decisions.

Suggested duration: 1 hour.

Participants: your leadership team.

Frequency: as often as your goal cycle planning.

> **Your organization is your team that will enable you to succeed.**
>
> **Building and strengthening your relevant value streams and capabilities will enable you to achieve your goals. The continuous development of your value streams and capabilities gives you more strategic flexibility, enabling you to engage in more challenging and valuable markets.**

To achieve the goals of their Apollo space program missions, NASA had to develop and adjust their organization. They made sure they had the right people, processes, information, tools and technologies in place. They did not build a helicopter, they built rockets and spacecraft. They built launching pads, fuel tanks, and everything needed to make the Moon landing happen.

By now, you have built your visible mission goals and metrics for the development or adjustment of your organization. This is what is needed to achieve your goals, which you defined during your 'Create Customer' process. Your 'Create Customer' goals and choices are informed by your business model, what you know about your competition, and your emerging future. The goals in your current goal cycle are steps on your vision roadmap.

In the next chapter, you will see how you bring everything together to monitor your organization (and roll with the 'punches' that inevitably come in the real world).

VALUE STREAM ASSESSMENT SHORTCUT

Prioritize your value streams by creating a chart like the one in Figure 106.

EL JEFE		Priority (5 point rating)					
Value Streams	**Responsible**	**Total**	**Truck**	**Miami**	**New Orleans**	**Austin**	**Los Angeles**
Health-Ready (cleaning)	Tony	**25**	5	5	5	5	5
Customer-to-Meal	Carl	**23**	3	5	5	5	5
Event-to-Permit	Carl	**20**	0	5	5	5	5
Work-to-Pay	Carl	**15**	3	3	3	3	3
Options-to-Events	Carl	**14**	0	2	3	4	5
Event-to-Awareness	Tony	**14**	0	2	3	4	5
Shopping-to-Ingredients	Carl	**13**	0	1	2	5	5
Use-to-Run (maint.)	Tony	**13**	5	2	2	2	2
Ingredient-to-Menu	Carl	**12**	0	1	2	4	5
Budget-to-Actual	Tony	**9**	1	2	2	2	2
Bill-to-Paid	Carl	**8**	0	2	2	2	2

Figure 106 – Prioritization chart (El Jefe)

To do your current state and future needs assessment of each value stream, create a chart like the one in Figure 107.

EL JEFE	Current State (5 point rating)					Future Need (5 point rating)				
Value Streams	**Total**	**Description**				**Total**	**Description**			
Health-Ready (cleaning)	**16**					**18**				
Customer-to-Meal	**18**					**19**				
Event-to-Permit	**10**					**15**				
Work-to-Pay	**20**					**20**				
Options-to-Events	**11**					**14**				
Event-to-Awareness	**8**					**12**				
Shopping-to-Ingredients	**8**					**12**				
Use-to-Run (maint.)	**7**					**9**				
Ingredient-to-Menu	**17**					**18**				
Budget-to-Actual	**15**					**15**				
Bill-to-Paid	**12**					**12**				

Figure 107 – Current state and future needs assessment (El Jefe)

Assuming that you create your charts in a spreadsheet, you can easily:

- create your matrices from the information, a
- calculate your value stream urgency score, and
- produce your urgency graph.

This is a fast way of doing your initial value stream analysis. It will not get you the quality of insights that you do when you go through the more detailed process. It will also not get you the highly valuable team buy-in that is often critical for helping you to succeed.

CHAPTER 17

Monitoring and Steering Your Visible Mission

The Moon landing was not conceived in NASA's Mission Control Center. But the Mission Control Center was where most of the Apollo space program's direction, execution, monitoring, and adjustments occurred to enable the Moon landing to ultimately succeed. It was where the missions in the Apollo space program originated, where they were executed, and where they were tracked to ensure success.

There were a number of failures along the way. For example, the Apollo 13 mission, and the accident on the launch pad in Apollo 1 was a tragic event. No mission control center could have undone those failures. In the same way, having a flawed business model, not effectively tracking your environment, picking the wrong customer initiatives, or not developing critical parts of your organization will not make you succeed.

But having your own fully functional mission control center (i.e. your visible mission) will help you to decide that it is better to abandon a particular mission (just like NASA did with Apollo 13) when the information (that you now have easy access to) calls for it. Not only that, it will help you to make better, more informed choices about business models, market selection, and the development of the organization you need to succeed, as well as help you track your way to success.

You now have:

- a vision and mission,
- a goal cycle,

- a clear view of your internal and external conditions,
- clear goal choices and metrics, and
- supporting capabilities to enable successful execution.

And now, you have a place and a process for monitoring your progress and making appropriate adjustments when necessary.

Tracking your progress is critical for reaching your goals. It allows you and your team to adjust your plans and actions based on the realities you face. Joint progress tracking also coordinates efforts, provides context to everyone, and strengthens the common purpose of your vision, mission and goals.

Having a wider perspective into your business models, industry, and major trends via your visible mission views will allow you to identify problems and opportunities earlier and more consistently. This in turn will help you to orient, decide, and be proactive.

You are here.

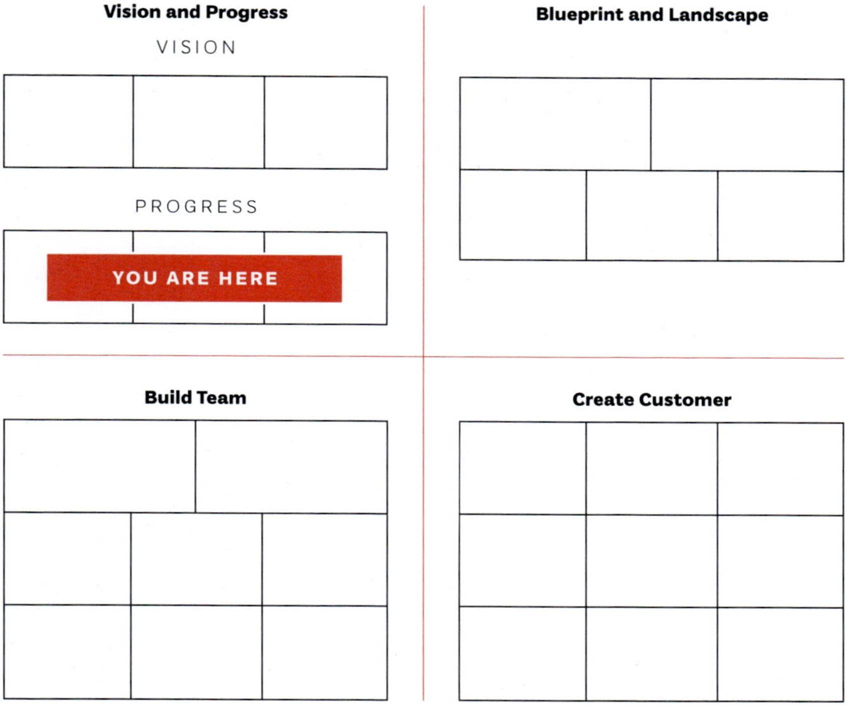

Figure 108 – You are here

REVIEWING YOUR PROGRESS

Recall from Chapter 9 that the progress section in the 'Vision and Progress' view of your visible mission has three components:

1) combined roadmap,

2) current status, and

3) progress.

Combined Roadmap

Your completed 'Build Team' roadmap from Chapter 16 should be appropriately aligned and coordinated with your 'Create Customer' roadmap.

Goals	Items	Dates			Calendar											
		Start	Target	Duration												

Figure 109 – Combined 'Create Customer' and 'Build Team' roadmap template

You will use this combined roadmap as part of your goal cycle monitoring. This is a reality check to see whether your team is completing initiatives on schedule. It is also a great tool to:

- orient yourself and your team.
- see how your planned progress compares to your actual progress (i.e. your current status).

Current Status

The best way to track your current status is to compare your actual vs. planned performance in three areas:

- metric,
- cost, and
- calendar.

I prefer to have each of these current status components expressed as a ratio to completion. For example:

- the progress towards achieving your metric may be something like a sales target (perhaps for a particular market and product). If your target is $100,000, and your current sales are $25,000, then your metric progress is 25%.
- if your expense/cost estimate for this sales target metric is $10,000 and you have spent $7,000 so far, you have spent 70% of your planned expense.

  In some activities, yo ur spending may either be front or back-loaded. The team responsible for the goal and/or metric should communicate such realities to the team. Front-loaded expenses may be the purchase of equipment, and back-loaded expenses may be where the payment for a contract may only happen at delivery.
- if you are 3 months into a planned 6-month activity, then that will show as 50%.
- your overall status in this example would be an average of all three ratios (i.e. 25% + 70% + 50%, divided by 3).

The goal of identifying your current status ratios is not to 'shake down' the team when there is a discrepancy. It is to create visibility and clear communication to enable you to steer effectively (for example, by assigning more resources, or helping out).

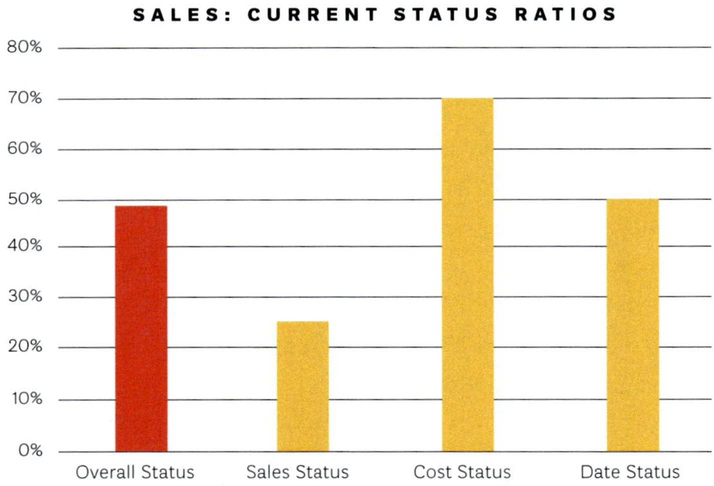

Figure 110 – Example of graphing current status ratios

Progress

While your current status reflects how you are performing right now, your progress reflects how you are performing over time. This 'view over time' helps you to identify when your intended initiatives (as expressed through the metrics) are stalling. For example, you may have some metrics that turn around. Let's say you have a target to add some number of customers a month. For a couple of months, you manage to do that, but then the numbers start falling. You want to be able to see this as soon as it starts happening so that you can investigate. Your current status at a single point in time will not show you this crucial information, however, a graph of your project trajectory will.

In Figure 111, we can see that the new customer goal (the green line) was flattening in July and August, which allowed us to identify corrective changes to our approach to implement in September and October to increase our number of new customers. The market share (gray line) and sales goals (orange lines) in this graph have moved along steadily.

It is also very useful to know how you are progressing overall. The yellow bar in Figure 111 indicates this overall progress. The intent is to get to or exceed 100% for all goals, or to get as close as possible.

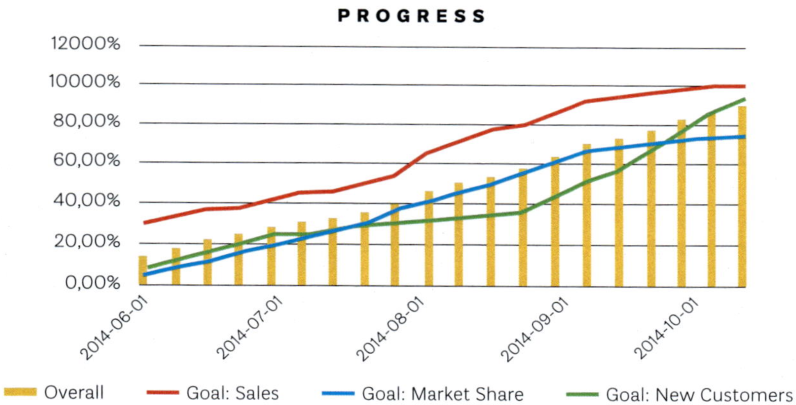

Figure 111 – Progress trajectory example

MONITORING AND STEERING

Chapter 11 outlined how you can use your visible mission to monitor and steer your organization. This should be an ongoing process, and to recap, the key components of the visible mission monitoring and steering process are:

- determining your meeting frequency (ideally weekly, but at least monthly).
- determining who should attend each meeting.
- scheduling your meetings.

- having an appropriate meeting agenda (that includes strategic developments, team progress reports, the making of necessary decisions, and the assigning of actions and responsibilities).

Monitoring and steering your visible mission is done with everyone in each relevant team involved and present. It is known as 'fishbowl management', since everyone can see what everyone else is doing. This creates a sense of common purpose, and it also shows the interdependencies of your work.

In addition, it ensures that people in your team get to share what they have accomplished, and what problems and roadblocks they have encountered.

A plan without monitoring means little.

To succeed, you have to execute your plan, monitoring both your progress and your unfolding realities. You can adjust your plans, priorities and resources as needed.

You are not putting your head in the sand, or complaining about the complexity of your situation. Instead, you are facing reality and the future head-on, and learning to use it to our advantage.

In a speech delivered on 12 September 1962, US president John F. Kennedy said: “We choose to go to the Moon (..), not because (it is) easy, but because (it is) hard.”

No amount of careful planning would have ensured that all NASA's missions worked as planned. Some were terrible failures. Yet, persistence, learning from failures, improving, and adjusting allowed NASA to make history on 20 July, 1969, when the Apollo 11 crew landed the lunar module named “Eagle” on the Moon. Four days later, the crew were safely back on Earth after having splashed down in the Pacific Ocean.

Your visible mission is your version of NASA's Mission Control Center. It will be clearly visible to you and your team, and it provides you with an approach that has helped other organizations to succeed. It is based on years of experience, learning from others, and is enriched by personal experience and failures.

You now have your own vision and mission, goal cycle, clear view of internal and external conditions, clear goals and metrics, as well as an enabling organization and capabilities. You have a process to enable you to monitor your progress and appropriately adjust when necessary. From here, you can define, inspire, guide, inform, collaborate, decide, act, adjust, and track your goals and initiatives through to completion.

Your visible mission will help you to gain perspective when there are too many things happening. It has a set of tools that will help you distinguish the important from the urgent. It can also help you and your team to come together to understand what to do when things go wrong. I hope that you and your team will use your visible mission to not only acknowledge the lessons you have to learn, but to celebrate your achievements in your ideas into plans, and your plans into reality.

It is my wish that you will use the visible mission to not only succeed with your own business, but to change the world. To make the world a better place for you, your children, and their children.

Conclusion

NASA's Mission Control Center was at the heart of turning the vision of a Moon landing into reality. It helped NASA to turn the vision into goals, the goals into plans and initiatives, and to monitor an evolving reality so that they could adjust and steer towards success.

Strategy management is neither rocket science nor voodoo.

You have seen first-hand that it is not as complicated as you might have thought, as you got to see and do it for yourself via creating your visible mission.

You have also seen how your visible mission will help you to survive by identifying and reacting to risks, as well as to thrive by identifying and exploiting opportunities.

It sets you up with a framework and provides you with tools to analyze information by understanding it within a relevant context. Your visible mission will help you to focus your attention and limited resources where they will make the most difference, and get you as ready as you need to be to reach your goals.

Your visible mission is an easy-to-use approach to imagine, analyze, plan, execute, and adjust to the evolving realities of your organization, your industry, and the world.

Part I of the book introduced the Good (how strategy management will help you to increase your chances of success and reduce your risk of failure); the Bad (why few CEOs actually manage strategy), and the Busy (how reacting uncritically to 'urgent' issues will undermine your ability to take care of what's most important).

In Part II, I shared the visible mission's structure with you. It makes strategy management easy. We stepped through creating your visible mission by looking at its four main views – 'Vision and Progress', 'Blueprint and Landscape', 'Create Customer', and 'Build Team'. For each of these views, you had the opportunity to note what information you already had in place, and what you needed to complete. At the end of Part II, we walked through how you could start steering your organization with what you have.

In Part III, we looked at the process of planning your visible mission and creating your vision roadmap. We saw how you could take a more structured approach to create your goal cycles, so they become more focused efforts to help you realize your vision. We started with your vision, goal cycle and assumptions. We then took a closer look at your organization's business model (the equivalent of an MRI scan), and a wider look at your environment (your radar) in terms of your industry assessment and emerging future landscapes.

This information provided the context for your 'Create Customer' work. Here we analyzed your customers, their problems, and how your products will solve their problems. Additionally, we examined your markets, goals, metrics and the initiatives you need to engage with your customers.

When digging deeper into your 'Build Team' view, I guided you through the identification and definition of your value streams, as well as their assessment and urgency. These insights enabled you to create goals and initiatives to build the organization you need to succeed in your current goal cycle, as well as preparing for your next one.

In the final chapter of Part III, we focused on arming your team with the strategic context of your work, and the importance of ongoing monitoring, steering and adjustments as you head towards success.

CALL TO ACTION: WHAT YOU SHOULD DO NOW

We are now at the end of the book. Even though you will put it down, I trust that you will continue to use your visible mission for yourself, your leadership team, and your larger team. Use it to:

- establish high-quality goals,
- develop a consistent record of highly effective execution, and
- create your own luck (by knowing where to be at the right time, and by being prepared to exploit opportunities).

If you haven't yet developed your visible mission as you have read through the book, I want you to start re-reading it at the beginning, and spend only 30 minutes each day with it. It doesn't matter whether you read it at the beginning of your work day, at the end, or somewhere in-between. It only needs to be at a time where you can turn off the fast-thinking associated with your operational responsibilities.

I want you to stop hitting the window for 30 minutes, and stand back. Then create one element of your visible mission. Tomorrow, create another one. 30 minutes. Every day. One chapter, or one section.

TIME EXPECTATION

To help you get an idea of a realistic time expectation for engaging with your visible mission, below is a guide. Keep in mind that the time you spend on this will more than be returned in terms of you:

a) picking the right opportunities,
b) avoiding threats appropriately,
c) not letting opportunities turn into threats,
d) better executing your initiatives,
e) developing the organization you need to succeed, and
f) focusing on what's really important (and not getting undermined by the 'urgent').

<table>
<tr><th rowspan="3">View</th><th rowspan="3">Element</th><th colspan="4">Time Spent</th><th rowspan="3">Frequency</th></tr>
<tr><th rowspan="2">Draft</th><th rowspan="2">Find</th><th colspan="2">Do</th></tr>
<tr><th>From</th><th>To</th></tr>
<tr><td rowspan="6">Visiond and Progress</td><td>Vision and Mission</td><td>0.5</td><td>0.5</td><td>1</td><td>8</td><td>Lifetime</td></tr>
<tr><td>Goal Cycle</td><td>0.5</td><td>0.5</td><td>1</td><td>2</td><td>Typically Annual</td></tr>
<tr><td>Assumptions</td><td>0.5</td><td>0.5</td><td>1</td><td>16</td><td>Ongoing</td></tr>
<tr><td>Roadmap</td><td>1</td><td>0.5</td><td>1</td><td>2</td><td>Monitor (Weekly, Monthly, etc.)</td></tr>
<tr><td>Status</td><td>1</td><td>0.5</td><td>1</td><td>2</td><td>Monitor (Weekly, Monthly, etc.)</td></tr>
<tr><td>Progress</td><td>1</td><td>0.5</td><td>1</td><td>2</td><td>Monitor (Weekly, Monthly, etc.)</td></tr>
<tr><td colspan="2"></td><td>4.5</td><td>3</td><td>6</td><td>32</td><td></td></tr>
<tr><td rowspan="5">Blueprint and Landscape</td><td>Business Model Naviagtor</td><td>1</td><td>0.5</td><td>1</td><td>20</td><td>Goal Cycle</td></tr>
<tr><td>Business Model Canvas</td><td>1</td><td>0.5</td><td>1</td><td>8</td><td>Goal Cycle</td></tr>
<tr><td>Industry Asssessment</td><td>1</td><td>0.5</td><td>1</td><td>8</td><td>Goal Cycle</td></tr>
<tr><td>Blue Ocean Strategy</td><td>1</td><td>0.5</td><td>1</td><td>8</td><td>Goal Cycle</td></tr>
<tr><td>Emerging Future</td><td>1</td><td>0.5</td><td>1</td><td>1</td><td>Ongoing</td></tr>
<tr><td colspan="2"></td><td>5</td><td>2.5</td><td>5</td><td>45</td><td></td></tr>
<tr><td rowspan="9">Create Customer</td><td>Customer Empathy Map</td><td>0.5</td><td>0.5</td><td>1</td><td>8</td><td>Goal Cycle, Ongoing</td></tr>
<tr><td>Value Proposition</td><td>0.5</td><td>0.5</td><td>4</td><td>8</td><td>Goal Cycle</td></tr>
<tr><td>Product</td><td>0.5</td><td>0.5</td><td>1</td><td>8</td><td>Goal Cycle, Ongoing</td></tr>
<tr><td>Geography</td><td>0.5</td><td>0.5</td><td>1</td><td>4</td><td>Goal Cycle</td></tr>
<tr><td>Market Segment</td><td>1</td><td>0.5</td><td>1</td><td>4</td><td>Goal Cycle</td></tr>
<tr><td>Market Segment Comparison</td><td>1</td><td>0.5</td><td>4</td><td>8</td><td>Goal Cycle</td></tr>
<tr><td>Goals and Metrics</td><td>1</td><td>0.5</td><td>4</td><td>8</td><td>Goal Cycle</td></tr>
<tr><td>Roadmap</td><td>2</td><td>0.5</td><td>4</td><td>8</td><td>Goal Cycle</td></tr>
<tr><td>Cost</td><td>1</td><td>0.5</td><td>2</td><td>4</td><td>Goal Cycle</td></tr>
<tr><td colspan="2"></td><td>8</td><td>4.5</td><td>22</td><td>60</td><td></td></tr>
<tr><td rowspan="8">Build Team</td><td>Value Streams</td><td>0.5</td><td>0.5</td><td>1</td><td>4</td><td>Goal Cycle, Ongoing</td></tr>
<tr><td>Key Resources (Functions)</td><td>1</td><td>0.5</td><td>2</td><td>8</td><td>Goal Cycle</td></tr>
<tr><td>Analysis</td><td>0.5</td><td>0.5</td><td>4</td><td>16</td><td>Goal Cycle</td></tr>
<tr><td>Matrix</td><td>0.5</td><td>0.5</td><td>1</td><td>2</td><td>Goal Cycle</td></tr>
<tr><td>Urgency</td><td>0.5</td><td>0.5</td><td>1</td><td>1</td><td>Goal Cycle</td></tr>
<tr><td>Goals and Metrics</td><td>1</td><td>0.5</td><td>4</td><td>8</td><td>Goal Cycle</td></tr>
<tr><td>Roadmap</td><td>1</td><td>0.5</td><td>4</td><td>8</td><td>Goal Cycle</td></tr>
<tr><td>Cost</td><td>1</td><td>0.5</td><td>4</td><td>8</td><td>Goal Cycle</td></tr>
<tr><td colspan="2"></td><td>6</td><td>4</td><td>21</td><td>55</td><td>Goal Cycle</td></tr>
</table>

Figure 112 – Time estimates for engaging with your visible mission

Keep in mind that as your visible mission becomes a standard part of your analysis, planning and operations, it will be subsumed within your regular work. For example, your customer empathy work should be part of what you do – it's not unique to strategic work, but it needs to happen. You will also get faster with basic visible mission work like your market comparisons, the creation and coordination of your roadmaps, etc.

Finally, as you use your visible mission, I would be delighted to hear from you. I'm very interested to learn from other practitioners. You can contact me via **www.henkjoubert.com/contact.html.**

Glossary

Capability

The *combination of people, process, information, tools and technologies to produce a particular outcome*. Example: customer management – all the elements to manage a customer from when they initially become a customer (e.g. via sales or marketing), when they pay, how they are supported, how they are targeted for new products, etc.

Development Initiative

Initiatives (and/or) *projects to improve the internal working of an organization* in terms of its value streams or capabilities. Example: redesigning a slow and ineffective value stream, and standardizing how to deal with product information across multiple systems.

Digitization

The *application of process, information, with an interface to enable automated capturing, processing, and responding to information*. Using computer systems to replace your paper system is not digitization on its own. Digitization is when you also use the digitization opportunity to standardize your business information by having (ideally) one version of an entity (e.g. a customer), and that information is integrated across all your systems (e.g. all the business areas who interact with your customer). You can also internally or externally digitize business processes with partners and customers.

Engagement Initiative

Initiatives (and/or) *projects to engage with a customer segment*, partner, product, or channel to achieve the strategic plan's business goals (i.e. strategic initiatives). I use the term 'engagement' based on military definitions of strategy (i.e. the choices of where, when, and how to engage with the opponent).

Strategy

The *choices of where, how, and when to engage with customers* through a combination of channels, products/value propositions, and customer relationship management activities, or to collaborate with business partners to achieve such an engagement. (Strategic choices dictate the terms of engagement that are suited to your strengths. For example, it is probably better to not try to compete with Amazon on the breadth of their inventory or logistics capabilities. Those are Amazon's strengths, and perhaps your organization's real presence, niche products with expert advice, or ability to provide a personal experience are your strengths.)

Value Stream

The *end-to-end processing to produce a complete and valuable product or service to a custome*r (internal or external). Example: Order to cash – all the activities from when an order is received, until it is paid for and fulfilled. Often, the individual steps in a value stream are optimized to the detriment of the entire value stream.

References

Blue Ocean Strategy: How to Create Uncontested Market Space and Make Competition Irrelevant – W Chan Kim, Renee Mauborgne (2005)

Business Model Generation: A Handbook for Visionaries, Game Changers, and Challengers – Alexander Osterwalder, Yves Pigneur (2010)

Competitive Strategy: Techniques for Analyzing Industries and Competitors – Michael E. Porter, 1998.

Doughnut Economics: Seven Ways to Think Like a 21st-Century Economist – Kate Raworth (2018)

Enterprise Architecture As Strategy: Creating a Foundation for Business Execution – Jeanne Ross, Peter Weil, David Robertson (2006)

Essential Advantage: *How to Win with a Capabilities-Driven Strategy* – Paul Leinwand, Cesare Mainardi (2010)

Lean UX: Designing Great Products with Agile Teams – Jeff Gothelf, Josh Seiden (2016)

Mapping Experiences: A Guide to Creating Value Through Journeys, Blueprints, and Diagrams – Jim Kalbach (2016)

Measure What Matters. OKRs: The Simple Idea that Drives 10x Growth – John Doerr (2017)

On War – Carl von Clausewitz, (Complete edition translated by J. J. Graham, 2018)

Playing to Win: How Strategy Really Works – A.G. Lafley, Roger L. Martin (2013)

Reengineering the Corporation: A Manifesto for Business Revolution – Michael Hammer, James Champy (2006)

The Black Swan: The Impact of the Highly Improbable: The Impact of the Highly Improbable –Nassim Nicholas Taleb (2010)

The Business Model Navigator: 55 Models that will Revolutionize Your Business – Oliver Gassmann, Karolin Frankenberger, Michaela Csik (2014)

The Great Transition: Using the Seven Disciplines of Enterprise Engineering to Align People, Technology, and Strategy – James Martin (1995)

The Innovator's Dilemma – Clayton Christensen (2016).

The Lean Startup: How Constant Innovation Creates Radically Successful Businesses – Eric Ries (2011)

The Outside-In Corporation – Barbara E. Bund (2014)

The Practice of Management – Peter Drucker (1986)

UX for Lean Startups: Faster, Smarter User Experience Research and Design – Laura Klein (2018)

Value Stream Mapping: How to Visualize Work and Align Leadership for Organizational Transformation – Karen Martin, Mike Osterlin (2013)

Wait: The Useful Art of Procrastination – Frank Partnoy (2013)